Brewing Made Easy

BREWING
Made Easy

A Step-by-Step Guide to Making Beer at Home

Second Edition

Joe Fisher & Dennis Fisher
authors of *The Homebrewer's Garden*

 Storey Publishing

*The mission of Storey Publishing is to serve our customers by
publishing practical information that encourages
personal independence in harmony with the environment.*

Edited by Margaret Sutherland and Sarah Guare
Art direction and book design by Alethea Morrison
Text production by Jennifer Jepson Smith
Cover and interior illustrations by © Scotty Reifsnyder
Indexed by Christine R. Lindemer, Boston Road Communications

Storey Publishing
210 MASS MoCA Way
North Adams, MA 01247
www.storey.com

Printed in the United States by Versa Press
10 9 8 7 6 5 4 3 2 1

LIBRARY OF CONGRESS CATALOGING-IN-PUBLICATION DATA
Fisher, Joe, 1966–
    Brewing made easy / Joe Fisher & Dennis Fisher. — 2nd edition.
        p. cm
    Includes index.
    ISBN 978-1-61212-138-3 (pbk. : alk. paper)
    ISBN 978-1-60342-854-5 (e-book)
    1. Brewing—Amateurs' manuals. I. Fisher, Dennis, 1963– II. Title.
TP570.F535 2013
641.8'73—dc23
                                                            2012032605

CONTENTS

YOU CAN BREW IT!

Every year tens of thousands of people become homebrewers. It isn't hard to get started. You just walk into your local brewstore and buy an equipment kit, a bag of brewing ingredients, and a book like this one. And then you start to brew. If you like what you made the first time, you brew again. And again.

Suddenly, you *are* a brewer, capable of creating any existing style of beer or of designing your own beers. You start to enter contests, join homebrewing clubs, subscribe to brewing magazines, grow your own hops, travel to conventions, and experience the exciting and growing world of beer from the best possible perspective: that of the brewing insider.

The reasons people have for brewing their own beer are many. But for most of us, it comes down to three essential goals: saving money, improving on flavor, and having fun.

SAVING MONEY. This is a great argument for making your own beer. Today an incredible variety of microbrews and imports is available, and there's nothing wrong with that! The fact that this country has finally thrown off the yoke of mediocre commercial beers and embraced the diversity of styles and good taste is cause for celebration. But many of these beers can be pricey. So why not make beer at home? You can brew simple extract beers such as we describe in this book for just fifty or sixty cents per glass. Compare that with import or brewpub prices! And all-grain brewers can achieve even greater savings. Of course, quality brewing ingredients are not cheap, nor should they be. But the sticker shock you may feel when picking up a big bag of brewstuff should be tempered by the knowledge that it will make a significant amount of beer.

IMPROVING ON FLAVOR. Most of us who brew at home feel that the taste of our beer is as good as, if not better than, anything on the market. We use the best ingredients and serve our beer perfectly fermented and aged. This is why homebrew is often superior to microbrew. Our beer doesn't have to be shipped anywhere, it doesn't sit on a shelf, and it doesn't have to make a profit. The only people our homebrew has to please are our friends, ourselves, and maybe a panel of judges if we decide to enter it in a contest. We can experiment with the amount and kinds of grain, the type of hops, or the strain of yeast. Ultimately, we can create a recipe that suits our palates perfectly, and it becomes our own *house beer*, something that we will brew again and again in the years to come.

HAVING FUN. Finally, brewing is fun. There is a deep satisfaction that comes from taking simple ingredients and combining, fermenting, and aging them to produce the age-old and ever-new libation called beer. Some people spend years perfecting just a few recipes; others never brew the same recipe twice. It all depends on what you want to do. Some brewers enjoy complex recipes and elaborate equipment setups; others cultivate simplicity. There is a comfort level of brewing for everybody. That's what makes homebrewing such a great hobby.

Brewing Made Easy is designed for the beginning brewer, and our goal has been to supply accurate, up-to-date information that is easy to understand and apply, so that you can start homebrewing right away, the right way. Every brewer does things a little differently, and over time you will undoubtedly develop an individual brewing style that suits you.

We wish you good luck and happy brewing!

Joe Fisher

Dennis Fisher

1

BREWING WITH MALT EXTRACTS

Malt extract brewing is the simplest way to make beer, and most people start out this way. Malt extract is the product of grain mashing, in which malt grains (barley that has been partially germinated, dried, and roasted to produce different brewing characteristics) are steeped at controlled temperatures to extract the brewing sugars. Then the resulting liquid is reduced until it is a syrup that contains only about 20 percent water.

Mashing is the trickiest stage of brewing, and using malt extracts means that you don't have to mash grain. Later, you can work up to more complex forms of brewing, such as partial mash and all grain. But for now, let's stick to the extracts.

Basic extract brewing is not complicated. Simply boil together malt extracts, either in syrup or dry form (often both are used in a recipe), water, and hops. You add hops to the brew (wort) at various stages of the boil to provide bitterness, flavor, and aroma. And finally you add yeast after the wort has cooled.

You can achieve even more simplicity by using can kits, which are cans of hopped malt extract formulated to make a particular beer. The recipe for Redemption Bitter (see page 15) is not much more complicated than a simple kit recipe, because it uses malt extract that has already been hopped by the manufacturer.

Basic Equipment

You will need a few pieces of basic equipment. If you buy a starter kit, much of what you need for basic brewing will be in it. In addition to what is shown at right, it's always handy to have a few white food-grade plastic buckets kicking around for cleaning bottles, soaking equipment, and so forth. Even the most occasional brewer will soon acquire a sizable collection of miscellaneous gear — and then he has to find room to store it! Our philosophy in writing this book has been to find the easiest method to help the beginner make good beer. To do this we will often recommend buying a desirable tool, such as a Vinator or Auto-Siphon, right away rather than waiting and using a simpler but sometimes less satisfactory method.

SANITIZE EVERYTHING!

The worst enemy of beer, and the most common cause of first-time-brewing failure, is contamination by microorganisms. The most important thing you can do for your beer is keep your brewing area clean and well sanitized. The standard in commercial breweries is close to operating-room cleanliness.

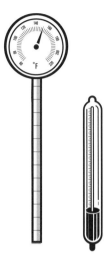

THERMOMETER. A thermometer, either a regular cooking thermometer (left) or a floating one (right), is useful for telling when it's safe to pitch the yeast. Yeast can stand very cold temperatures, but anything above 90°F will kill it.

BREW POT.
A 16-quart stainless steel pot is fine for basic extract brewing.

FERMENTATION LOCK. A clear plastic airlock allows carbon dioxide to escape during fermentation but keeps air from reaching your beer.

PLASTIC FERMENTING BUCKET WITH LID.
A 6.7-gallon plastic fermenter usually comes with the equipment kit.

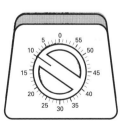

LONG-HANDLED METAL OR PLASTIC STIRRING SPOON.

MEDIUM-SIZE STAINLESS STEEL STRAINER. A metal strainer is useful for rinsing grains and straining spent hops from wort.

TIMER. A kitchen timer helps you keep track of boiling times. Not essential — but definitely helpful.

This is necessary because beer-loving bacteria and wild yeast colonies build up wherever beer is present. Always wipe down the brewing area with a rag soaked in sanitizing solution before and after you brew.

When we started brewing we used a bleach solution to sanitize everything. Bleach is hard on the environment (and your body) and needs to be rinsed off thoroughly; luckily, other options are now available. We like to make up a couple of gallons of Star San solution in a spare plastic bucket and soak our equipment in it while boiling the wort. It takes only a minute or so of contact with Star San to kill microorganisms, and it doesn't need to be rinsed off, which eliminates the possibility of contamination during rinsing. You can take your spoon out of the solution, stir your wort, and put it right back in without missing a beat. It's also biodegradable and odorless.

Star San is long lasting in solution form and can be reused several times. If it's not cloudy and foams up when agitated, we feel comfortable using it again. If diluted with deionized water, Star San solution can keep for 2 or 3 months. An 8-ounce bottle will make 32 gallons of solution, and it's pretty cheap. The writing on the bottle is tiny, and the bottle itself is a little tricky. Remove the left-hand cap and gently squeeze the bottle to fill the small reservoir on top to the desired level. Because Star San is an acid-based product, it can leave rings on some countertops and can be hard on rubber, so it may affect some of your equipment after a period of use.

Cleansers and Sanitizers

All equipment must be clean before it can be sanitized. The following are just some of the options you have for cleansers and sanitizers.

BAKING SODA. Sodium bicarbonate is a nontoxic abrasive cleanser (not a sanitizer) that can be used to clean beer equipment such as carboys and brew pots.

IODOPHOR. This iodine-based sanitizer is effective for all types of brewing equipment. It is unlikely to produce any off-flavors. It requires no rinsing when diluted to correct concentration.

ONE STEP. No rinsing is necessary when using this oxygen-based environmentally friendly cleanser/sanitizer. Dissolve 1 tablespoon of One Step in 1 gallon of warm water.

PBW (POWDERED BREWERY WASH). This alkali-based cleanser is used to remove stubborn brewing deposits. It also removes labels from beer bottles. Dissolve 1 ounce of PBW in 1 gallon of hot water and soak equipment overnight to clean.

STAR SAN. This acid-based foaming sanitizer is odorless and flavorless and will not produce off-flavors. It sanitizes surfaces and equipment after 1 to 2 minutes of exposure. Dilute at a rate of ¼ ounce Star San to 1 gallon of cold water.

Brewing at a Glance

1. Sanitize your plastic fermenter bucket, lid, long-handled spoon, fermentation lock, strainer, and thermometer in a solution of water and Star San (1 gallon of water to ¼ ounce Star San).

2. Add 1½ gallons of cold water to your fermenting bucket.

3. Immerse the unopened can of malt extract in warm water.

4. Heat 1½ gallons of cold water enough to melt malt extracts (100–120°F).

5. Add malt extracts to the hot water and boil according to recipe. Add flavoring hops as required. Bring ½ gallon of rinse water to a boil.

6. Turn off heat and add aroma hops.

7. Pour boiled wort through strainer into fermenter. Rinse hops with boiled water.

8. Add cold water to make 5 gallons.

9. When wort has cooled to around 70°F, pitch the yeast.

10. Attach fermentation lock and cover.

11. Ferment for 7 to 10 days.

12. Prime, bottle, and cap.

The First Recipe

For our first batch of beer, we are going to make a simple extract bitter. Bitter is the standard English pub beer and is a favorite of ours because it has a lot of character, despite its simplicity. Your basic "ordinary" bitter is moderate in alcohol and reddish gold in color, and can express a wide range of bitterness. The emphasis in this style is on the bittering hops. It's popular with homebrewers because it's fast and easy to brew. It is not a long-keeping beer, so you can brew it, drink it up, and make some more.

Redemption Bitter

All of these ingredients can be purchased at any brewstore.

INITIAL GRAVITY: 1.039–1.045
FINAL GRAVITY: 1.014–1.016

- 3.3 pounds (1.5 kg) amber hopped malt extract syrup

- 2 pounds (907 g) plain light dry malt extract

- 1 ounce (28 g) East Kent Goldings flavoring hops

- ½ ounce (14 g) East Kent Goldings aroma hops

- 1 packet Fermentis Safale S-33 ale yeast

- ½ cup (120 ml) corn sugar or ¾ cup (180 ml) dry malt extract for priming

1. Sanitize your plastic fermenting bucket, lid, long-handled spoon, fermentation lock, strainer, and thermometer in a solution of Star San (¼ ounce [7.4 ml] per 1 gallon [3.8 L] water). Mix the sanitizing solution in a separate 5-gallon (19 L) food-grade plastic bucket. Pour ½ gallon (1.9 L) into the fermenter bucket, seal with the lid, and slosh it around until the sides of the bucket and bottom of the lid are coated in foam. Return any unused solution to the mixing bucket and place the rest of your equipment in it. A few minutes of immersion should sanitize it thoroughly.

Step 5

2. Add 1½ gallons (5.7 L) cold water to the fermenting bucket. Seal with the lid and set aside.

3. Immerse the unopened can of malt extract in hot water for about 10 minutes to make it easier to work with. Trim off the top of the plastic bag of dry malt extract. This prevents steam from hydrating the extract and causing a sticky mess.

4. Heat 1½ gallons (5.7 L) of cold water in the brew pot to a high enough temperature to melt the malt extracts (100–120°F/38–49°C).

5. Remove the brew pot from the heat. Pour the hopped malt extract into the brew pot and scrape any remaining syrup away from the sides of the can. Add the dry malt extract and stir well to dissolve. Return the brew pot to the heat and boil for 30 minutes.

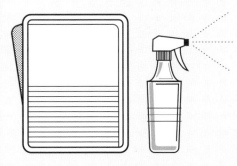

Other Useful Tools

A SANITIZED, DEDICATED PAINT TRAY makes an excellent spot to rest your thermometer, long spoon, and strainer between uses. It is much easier to sanitize than, for instance, a dish rack.

A SPRAY BOTTLE full of sanitizing solution is useful both for sanitizing surfaces around the brewing area and sanitizing equipment that is too large or awkward to dip in the solution bucket.

6. Add the flavoring hops. These will contribute flavor and aroma to the finished beer.

7. Remove the brew pot from the heat when the wort has boiled for 45 minutes, and add the aroma hops. Cover the pot and steep for 5 minutes. Allow the brew pot to cool until it can be safely handled.

8. Carefully pour the boiled wort through the strainer and into the fermenter.

9. Rinse the spent hops with ½ gallon (1.9 L) 180°F (82°C) water.

10. Add enough cold water to make 5 gallons (19 L). (On a standard primary fermenter bucket, the 5-gallon mark is indicated by the thick plastic collar. It is also useful to mark gallon increments on the outside of the bucket with a permanent marker.) Stir thoroughly with the sanitized spoon to mix the water with the wort.

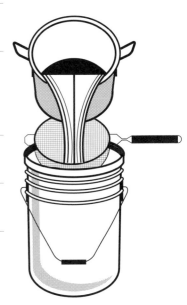

Step 8

11. Measure the temperature of the wort. It needs to cool down to around 70°F (21°C) before you can add the yeast. Be sure to rinse the thermometer and shake it down; otherwise, it will give you a false reading. Temperatures of 90°F (32°C) and up are fatal to yeast; temperatures between 60°F and 70°F (15.5–21°C) are ideal for ales (a few degrees above or below that range is fine); lower temperatures are necessary for lagers.

12. Add the yeast and stir in gently with the sanitized spoon.

Step 12

13. Attach the fermenter lid and the fermentation lock. The fermentation lock must be filled with water. (The gasket in the lid is usually a pretty tight fit for the stem of the airlock. It helps to push against the gasket from the underside of the lid while twisting the airlock.)

14. Allow to ferment for 7 to 10 days in a quiet spot, out of direct light, at temperatures between 60°F and 70°F (15.5–21°C) for ale, or between 45°F and 50°F (7–10°C) for lager.

15. Prime, bottle, and cap the beer once the fermentation is complete. Priming (page 24) is a necessary step for carbonation. This chore goes a lot faster if you have two people: one to fill the bottles and one to cap. From setup to cleanup, priming and bottling usually takes only an hour or so.

Step 13

Is It Beer Yet?

The airlock, or fermentation lock, can be used to tell if the beer is finished. If bubbles have stopped coming out of the airlock, or if they appear only once every 90 seconds or longer, then the beer is ready to bottle.

If your beer is an ale, you should see yeast activity within 24 hours. Bubbles released by the fermentation lock will tell you that your wort is fermenting. Eventually, the bubbles will stop completely. A good rule of thumb is to allow the beer to sit for a few days after fermentation ceases before bottling, to allow the beer to "drop clear" — that is, for the yeast to become dormant and sink to the bottom of the fermenter.

Bottle Hygiene

You can acquire bottles new and clean from your homebrew store, or get them used from the redemption center. We usually use brown 12-ounce beer bottles, but we are partial to any bail-top or 22-ounce or larger bottles that come our way. With old bail-tops you may have to replace the gaskets. Used bottles can be pretty scummy and will at least have to be rinsed out. A good way to get bottles clean is to soak them for a couple of days in brewery wash (PBW). This not only gets rid of any dried-on sediment but will even scour off the old labels. Rinse them thoroughly before sanitizing. Any tough spots can be scrubbed with a bottle brush. If a bottle is still not squeaky clean after this treatment, it gets recycled.

Always rinse out your bottles after use! This habit will make it much easier to clean them the next time around. We store ours between uses in heavy-duty wax produce boxes in the cellar, with a piece of cloth thrown over them to keep out dust and spiders.

Ingredients for Priming Beer

CORN SUGAR. Homebrew supply shops carry corn sugar for brewers. The corn sugar is used to prime the beer by giving the yeast an extra bit of food to digest while it is in the bottle.

UNFLAVORED GELATIN (optional). Gelatin is a fining or clarifying agent. Adding unboiled gelatin to the priming solution removes small particles of protein and yeast residues from the beer.

Bottling Equipment

For bottling, you will need the following equipment.

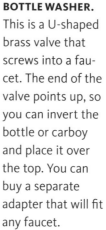

50 EMPTY LONG-NECKED BEER BOTTLES. Use long-necked bottles that require an opener. The bottles should be brown; clear or green ones will admit too much light, giving your beer a skunky aroma.

AUTO-SIPHON. This plastic siphon is useful for racking beer to the bottling bucket or secondary fermenter. It comes in several different sizes.

LONG-HANDLED SPOON. Use a metal spoon. It will be the easiest kind to sanitize.

BOTTLE WASHER. This is a U-shaped brass valve that screws into a faucet. The end of the valve points up, so you can invert the bottle or carboy and place it over the top. You can buy a separate adapter that will fit any faucet.

CAPPER. The wing capper shown here is a two-levered design.

BOTTLE CAPS. Ordinary crown caps work fine for bottling beer and are readily available at homebrew supply shops.

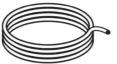

PLASTIC TUBING. A short length of ½-inch tubing comes with the equipment kit. You may find that longer tubing is easier to use.

SAUCEPANS. You will need these to prepare the priming solution and gelatin.

FILLER WAND. This is a plastic tube with a spring valve at one end.

PLASTIC BOTTLING BUCKET WITH SPIGOT. Equipment kits usually come with a bottling bucket. It can also be used as a secondary fermenter in a two-stage fermentation, which we will talk about in chapter 2.

VINATOR. This plastic bottle washer that operates by hand-pumping is inexpensive, effective, and fun to use.

Bottling Your First Batch

1. **SANITIZE THE EQUIPMENT.** Mix up a 1-gallon batch of Star San in a bucket. Soak your plastic bottling bucket, plastic tubing, and filler wand in sanitizing solution for at least 30 minutes. If you are using Star San, no rinsing is necessary.

   If you are using a bottling bucket, sanitize the spigot. Securely attach the filler wand and plastic tubing to the spigot.

2. **SANITIZE THE BOTTLES.** You can't sanitize something that isn't clean, so make sure your bottles are clean before moving on to this step (see box, page 19). Add some sanitizing solution to your Vinator. Invert a bottle over the top of the Vinator and pump up and down a few times to thoroughly coat the inside of the bottle. Set the bottle down upright and do the next one. You should do only a half dozen at a time to keep them from drying out before they're filled. Just before filling, turn the bottle upside down and give it a shake to get rid of any extra sanitizer.

   If you decide not to invest in a Vinator right away, you can sanitize the bottles by dunking them into a bucket of Star San, making sure that they get completely coated inside, and then emptying them out.

Step 2

3. **SANITIZE THE BOTTLE CAPS.** There are many different ways to do this, but this method is what we recommend. Take a pint glass of Star San solution and put all of your bottle caps in it. As you fill the bottles, you can set a bottle cap on each one to prevent anything from falling into it. When all the bottles are filled, seal them with the capper. A warning about doing this: If you are using oxygen-fixing bottle caps, they are good only for about 10 minutes after they get wet, so this method won't work with them. But the yeast remaining in the beer will remove any oxygen in the bottle as it works, so getting your caps well sanitized is really more important than their oxygen-reducing potential.

4. **SIPHON THE FERMENTED BEER** from the fermenter into the sanitized bottling bucket.

   Place the fermenter higher than the empty, sanitized bucket (see diagram, right).

   Many basic equipment kits now come with an Auto-Siphon, and we recommend that new brewers use this tool for siphoning from the fermenter to the bottling bucket, a process called "racking." They come in a number of sizes, so get one for use with a 5-gallon bucket or carboy. The Auto-Siphon is easy to use, much more so than older methods of siphoning, and is less prone to contamination because you never touch the beer.

   Sanitize the unit thoroughly with Star San and attach a length (5 to 6 feet) of sanitized tubing. Lower the Auto-Siphon about halfway into the liquid (to avoid bottom sediments) and give it a couple of pumps. The siphon will start easily. If an air bubble develops or the

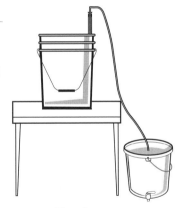

Step 4

Step 5

Step 7

siphon quits, just pump it a few more times. Now, holding it diagonally, carefully lower the Auto-Siphon to the bottom of the fermenter. The cap at the base will keep out sediment. The process is hands free at this point and you can do something else while the siphoning progresses. You can also remove this cap to get more beer out, holding the Auto-Siphon just above the sediments.

Priming

Before you bottle, you will be "priming" the beer, which simply means adding sugar to the beer. Priming helps to carbonate the beer, by giving the yeast an extra bit of food (the sugar) to digest while it's in the bottle.

The kind of sugar you want to use for priming is dextrose (corn sugar), rather than sucrose (cane sugar). Corn sugar is more readily fermented than household cane sugar and not so inclined to produce a "cidery"-tasting beer.

Note: Even corn sugar should not be used in excessive amounts, or the beer will suffer.

5. **ADD ¾ CUP (180 ML) CORN SUGAR** to 2 cups (475 ml) water to make the priming solution. Stir to dissolve, and bring to a boil.

6. **HEAT ¼ OUNCE OF UNFLAVORED GELATIN** in 2 cups (475 ml) water. Do not boil. Stir to dissolve.

7. **ADD THE PRIMING SOLUTION AND GELATIN SOLUTION** to the beer. Stir gently with a sanitized spoon.

8. **MOVE THE NOW-FULL BOTTLING BUCKET** to a higher position so that gravity will help the beer to flow. Attach plastic tubing to the bottling bucket spigot. Assemble the sanitized filler wand and attach it to the plastic tubing. Open the spigot.

9. **FILL THE BOTTLES.** Press the filler wand against the bottom of the bottle to release beer. Lift up to shut off the flow. Leave approximately 1 inch of headspace in the bottle.

Step 9

10. **PLACE A CAP ON THE BOTTLE** so it sits evenly. Bring the handles of the capper together, so the jaws meet around the neck of the bottle. Push the handles apart until the cap seats. Now release. The cap will attach, and the weight of the bottle will pull it away from the capper.

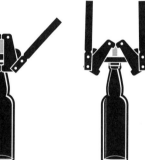

Step 10

Beer ID

A simple way to identify beer is just to write the beer name initials and date on plain bottle caps with a magic marker: For instance, Monitor Doppelbock brewed on June 19, 2013, would be written "M.D. 6-19-13." Then you can note what beer the initials refer to on a list tacked up on a wall in your beer cellar.

Store and Age

Use cardboard case boxes to hold your beer (most home-brew batches will make two cases). Beer stores best in a cool, dark place, such as a cellar. Beers must be aged to allow natural carbonation to take place. Some of the flavors of beer will subtly change with aging. However you choose to age your homebrew, it's a good idea to allow it to carbonate in a warm place (68–72°F) for a week or so before moving it to storage temperature. Ales will generally be ready to drink in 2 to 6 weeks. Lagers should be aged for at least 1 to 2 months. A high-quality homebrew is the result of several factors — initial specific gravity, alcohol content, and hoppiness being only the most obvious. Low-gravity 'session' beers such as English Bitter and Dunkel are best if consumed soon after carbonation is complete, while high-gravity, heavily hopped Barleywine Ale and Belgian Tripel come to perfection only after years in the cellar.

Cheers!

2 THE SECOND BATCH

Now that you've experienced brewing a basic extract beer, you can try something a little more complicated. In this chapter we'll talk about adding grains to beer and discuss the use of some more advanced equipment that can make your brewing experience even easier. None of the equipment or materials we talk about here is particularly expensive or involved, especially when compared with some of the setups you see for all-grain brewing. The recipe we present here is also a bitter, like the recipe in chapter 1. Later on in the recipe section we often give two versions of the styles we cover, one simple and one a little more complicated — but still pretty easy!

Intermediate Brewing at a Glance

1. Sanitize your carboy, wine thief, stopper, long-handled spoon, fermentation lock, strainer, funnel, thermometer, plastic tube, and hydrometer in a solution of water and Star San ($\frac{1}{4}$ ounce Star San to 1 gallon water).

2. Add $1\frac{1}{2}$ gallons of cold water to your carboy.

3. Crush grains and put them in a grain bag.

4. Heat $1\frac{1}{2}$ gallons of water to about 150°F. Bring $\frac{1}{2}$ gallon rinse water to a boil.

5. Add grains to carboy and steep for 15 minutes. Gently squeeze as much liquid as possible from the grain bag using a spoon.

6. Place the grain bag in a strainer and rinse with the $\frac{1}{2}$ gallon 180°F rinse water.

7. Add malt extracts and bittering hops and boil according to recipe. Add flavoring hops as required. Bring $\frac{1}{2}$ gallon rinse water to a boil.

8. Turn off heat and add aroma hops. Steep for 5 minutes.

9. Pour boiled wort through strainer into fermenter. Rinse hops with the $\frac{1}{2}$ gallon 180°F rinse water.

10. Add cold water to make 5 gallons.

11. Take a sample of your wort with the wine thief. Take a hydrometer reading.

12. When wort has cooled to around 70°F, pitch the yeast.

13. Attach stopper and blow-by hose.

14. When fermentation dies down, remove blow-by and attach fermentation lock.

15. Ferment for 7 to 10 days.

16. When fermentation stops, take a second hydrometer reading.

17. Prime, bottle, and cap.

Equipment

Intermediate brewing requires the addition of a few new tools to the brew kit. Some of these aren't strictly necessary, but all of them will make your brewing a bit easier. In this chapter we talk about using a carboy as a fermenter in place of the plastic bucket. Some "deluxe" kits come with glass carboys, or you can buy them separately. Unlike the plastic bucket fermenter, glass will never get scratched and is easier to get clean; most brewers end up owning a bunch of them. There is a place for bucket-type fermenters in advanced brewing, though, especially if you are adding fruit, which is difficult to stuff down through the narrow neck of a carboy, and equally hard to get out again. When brewing very hoppy beers such as the newly popular superhopped IPAs, it's common to stick with a bucket fermenter to keep from losing hop character when the krausen exits the carboy through the blow-by system (see box, page 38).

HYDROMETER AND PLASTIC HYDROMETER TUBE. The hydrometer is a graduated glass instrument that measures the specific gravity (density) of your wort.

KETTLES. Enamelware canners or stainless steel pots can be used as boiling kettles. Avoid plain steel and iron — they can give your beer a metallic taste. A 2-gallon pot is useful for steeping malt grains.

(continued on next page)

(continued from previous page)

CARBOY. This is a large, transparent glass bottle used as a fermenter. Plastic carboys are also available, which have the advantage of being much lighter and less fragile.

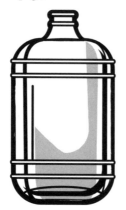

BOTTLE BRUSH AND CARBOY BRUSH. These are used for cleaning bottles and scrubbing out the top of the carboy.

FUNNEL. A large plastic funnel is very useful when you start fermenting in a carboy. It should be big enough to hold your strainer.

GRAIN BAG. Grain bags make it easier to add grains to the brew pot.

HOP BAG. Similar to a grain bag, a hop bag is used for confining dry hops in the secondary fermenter.

Plastic Carboys

A new wrinkle in brewing is the plastic carboy. These are light, inexpensive, and practically unbreakable. We love our glass carboys, but I've also had one disintegrate in my hands after a light tap on the sink. This won't happen with plastic. Some kits come with plastic carboys now, or you can buy them separately. You can clean and sanitize them like a glass carboy, but use a soft bottle brush to prevent scratches. As with any plastic fermenter, discard when you start to see scratches, because microorganisms can hide in them and affect your beer.

GRAIN MILL. Most homebrew stores will have an electric grain mill, so you can have the grain crushed there, but home mills are also available.

NOTEBOOK. A beer notebook is a valuable resource. Use it to keep track of when you brewed, what ingredients you used, how long you boiled, how long the beer took to ferment, any problems you encountered, when you bottled, and how you liked the beer. Writing down your observations and procedures will allow you to reproduce any beers you especially liked (or avoid problems) in the future.

STOPPER. You should have two rubber stoppers for your carboy: one with a hole in it to allow for the blow-by hose and fermentation lock, and a solid one for those times when you need to stop the neck of the carboy. Plastic carboy caps are also inexpensive, easy to use, and durable. The straight connector is used for the airlock, while the angled connector attaches to the blow-by hose.

PLASTIC TUBING. Clear plastic tubing, ½ to ¾ inch in diameter, is invaluable to the intermediate homebrewer, not only for siphoning beer from the fermenter to the carboy and connecting the filler wand to the bottling bucket, but for removing krausen as part of a blow-by system and connecting the carbon dioxide tank to the keg.

WINE THIEF. A plastic tube with a gravity valve at one end, it is useful for taking samples of wort for hydrometer readings.

Diamond Jubilee Extra Special Bitter

INITIAL GRAVITY: 1.042–1.050
FINAL GRAVITY: 1.012–1.015

- 2 ounces (56 g) Midnight Wheat or English Chocolate malt
- 10 ounces (280 g) 60° Lovibond English Crystal malt
- 4 pounds (1.8 kg) John Bull Best Bitter kit
- 2 pounds (907 g) dry extra light malt extract
- 1½ ounces (42 g) Northern Brewer bittering hops
- ½ ounce (14 g) East Kent Goldings flavoring hops
- ½ ounce (14 g) Fuggles flavoring hops
- ½ ounce (14 g) East Kent Goldings aroma hops
- ½ ounce (14 g) Willamette aroma hops
- 1 packet Wyeast #1968 London ESB or Fermentis Safale S-04 ale yeast
- ⅔ cup (160 ml) corn sugar, for priming

1. Sanitize your equipment as described in chapter 1 (see page 10). Pour ½ gallon (1.9 L) of Star San solution into the carboy and seal with the stopper. Slosh it around until the inside is completely covered in foam. Return the excess sanitizer to the bucket.

2. Add 1½ gallons (5.7 L) of cold water to your carboy. Secure the funnel in the neck of the carboy first. Never pour hot wort directly into an empty carboy, as heat stress can cause the carboy to shatter. The water should be cold enough to promote a good cold break even if it hasn't been chilled.

3. Put crushed grains in a grain bag. If you haven't bought them precrushed, you can crush the grains with a grain mill or a rolling pin. Put them inside a plastic freezer bag, lay the bag on a flat surface, and use a rolling pin or can to crack the grains. Grain bags are mesh bags used to contain grains while steeping, somewhat like a giant tea bag. This makes it easier to handle the grains and allows you to use just one pot for the operation. Pour the malt grains into the bag and tie off the neck.

4. Heat 1½ gallons (5.7 L) of water to about 150°F (65.5°C). Bring ½ gallon (1.9 L) rinse water to a boil. We use a 2-gallon (7.6 L) stainless steel pot. In a separate saucepan, boil ½ gallon (1.9 L) of water for rinsing.

5. Add the grains and steep for 15 minutes. Beers with a heavier malt bill, such as Imperial stouts and barleywine-style ales, may require a longer steep for up to 30 minutes. (Do not boil the grains.) The grains will swell up in the pot. Gently squeeze as much liquid as possible from the grain bag using a spoon.

Step 5

6. Place the grain bag in a strainer and rinse with the ½ gallon (1.9 L) 180°F (82°C) rinse water. Pour some of the rinsing water into the strainer and press down on the grains with the spoon to extract the liquid from the malt. Now you can add the malt extracts to the strained liquid and proceed with your brewing.

7. Add the malt extract syrup as discussed in chapter 1 (see page 9) and stir until completely dissolved. Bring the wort to a rolling boil and add the bittering hops. While the wort is boiling, proteins will coagulate and rise to the top, forming a whitish scum called "trub." Skim off this layer using a long-handled spoon. This results in a clearer beer. Some brewers recommend waiting until after trub has ceased to appear to add the hops, to allow better hop utilization and avoid skimming off the hops with the trub.

Step 6

Step 7

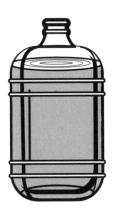

Step 10

When the wort has boiled for 45 minutes, add the flavoring hops. Bring ½ gallon (1.9 L) rinse water to a boil. Boil for 15 minutes longer.

8. Turn off the heat and add the aroma hops. Allow to steep for 5 minutes. At this point the wort will be hot enough to sanitize the hops, but not so hot as to drive off the delicate hop aromas.

   Hot wort is difficult and messy to pour out of a brew pot. Setting the pot in a cold-water bath can cool it off faster, as can setting it outside in a snowbank if you're lucky enough to have one. The brew pot should be cool enough to handle comfortably before the wort is poured into the fermenter.

9. Pour the boiled wort through a strainer into the fermenter. Rinse hops with ½ gallon (1.9 L) 180°F (82°C) water.

10. Add cold water to make 5 gallons (19 L). The 5-gallon mark on a standard carboy is the point where the "shoulders" begin to taper toward the neck.

Cold-Water Bath

Immersing the fermenter in a cold-water bath can help to quickly bring down the wort temperature.

11. Take a sample of the wort using your sanitized sample tube or wine thief. Cool it to 60°F (15.5°C) and take a hydrometer reading (see Appendix B: How to Use the Hydrometer, page 97). This is your initial specific gravity, which should be close to the specified initial gravity listed with the recipe ingredients.

12. When the wort has cooled to around 70°F (21°C), pitch the yeast.

13. Attach blow by tube (see box on p. 00 for information on using the blow-by system.) Set the carboy and milk jug on a large flat receptacle such as a jelly roll pan to contain any overflow from vigorous fermentation. Fit the sanitized plastic tube into the neck of the carboy. Put the free end of the tube into the milk jug. The whole thing forms an air lock.

14. When fermentation dies down, remove the blow-by and attach the fermentation lock.

15. Ferment for 7 to 10 days.

16. When fermentation stops, take a second hydrometer reading.

17. Bottle and cap.

Checking the Specific Gravity

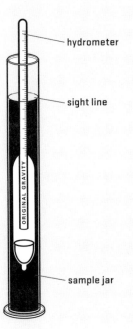

hydrometer

sight line

ORIGINAL GRAVITY

sample jar

Beginning brewers are always happy to have a way to see that things are going right with a recipe, and checking the specific gravity (beer density) is a good way to do that. By accurately measuring the specific gravity, you can determine (1) when the yeast has finished fermenting, and (2) the amount of alcohol in the beer.

Gravity is checked with a hydrometer, the little glass instrument that comes with a brew kit. It's actually pretty easy to do, and it's an extra step that can help ensure brewing success every time.

You ordinarily use the hydrometer twice in basic brewing: first to test the specific gravity of the unfermented wort (initial gravity), and second to find the specific gravity of the finished beer (final gravity). The initial reading is taken after the wort has been topped off up to 5 gallons — but before the yeast is pitched — and gives the brewer an idea of the amount of fermentable material in the wort. The second reading is used to confirm that fermentation is complete.

Primary and Secondary Fermentation

Primary fermentation is the first, explosive phase of fermentation, usually taking just a few days, and secondary fermentation is a more sedate stage that can take weeks. The point of secondary fermentation is to move beer to a second vessel to get it off the spent yeast, settled proteins, and other decaying matter that have settled in the wort. Therefore, using a secondary fermenter (especially a glass one) can really help improve the clarity and flavor of beer. "Racking" the beer simply means to transfer it by siphoning to a sanitized secondary fermenter, either the one provided with your equipment set or a glass carboy. Beer styles that ferment completely in a short time, such as low-gravity styles and most British ales, may not require racking off to a secondary fermenter, because the time between pitching the yeast and bottling the beer is relatively short. That's why we don't discuss using a secondary fermentation for this ESB, though you can do it if you want to.

On the other hand, high-gravity ales such as Belgian Triple and brandywine-style ale, as well as any style of lager, benefit greatly from long fermentation in the secondary. How long depends on the style and strength of the beer and on what you are trying to accomplish. Lagers, if fermented at proper cold lagering temperatures, will take a lot longer to ferment anyway, and they might as well do this off of the old sediments from primary fermentation.

Another factor to consider is the type of yeast used to ferment a particular batch. Dried yeast will have a certain amount of dead yeast cells in it to begin with, which will sink to the bottom of the fermenter and cause off-flavors if the beer is allowed to sit on them. Liquid yeast, provided it has been properly refrigerated, will be full of lively, vigorous yeast cells that will take off quickly and not cause problems later on. However, highly flocculent yeast strains (see box on page 54) of either type will create a lot of sediment when they do settle out, and highly hopped beers will have hop residues that would be better left behind in the primary fermenter.

Personally, we rarely use secondary fermentation — it's just easier not to and we are always pretty happy with the results we achieve. Our brewguy Asa puts it this way: he tells new brewers always to use a secondary at first. This helps get a consistent product and teaches patience, something any home-brewer can use. Later on, as the brewer grows in experience and skill, Asa suggests when the practice can be omitted and when it is appropriate, based on factors such as style, yeast selection, and so forth.

After pitching the yeast, fit the end of the tubing into the neck of the carboy and place the other end in the milk jug. Replace the blow-by with an airlock and stopper when the primary fermentation is complete.

The Blow-by System

The blow-by system is a standard homebrewing technique, important during primary fermentation, when the beer produces a huge foamy head, or krausen. In the bucket-type primary fermenter, the krausen cannot escape and eventually sinks back into the beer. This can contribute off-flavors to the homebrew. The only way to get rid of it is to open the fermenter and scoop up the brownish foam with a sanitized spoon, but this can allow microorganisms a chance to get at your beer and spoil it.

The blow-by gets around this problem by allowing much of the krausen to escape the fermenter through the plastic tube. To put together a blow-by setup, you will need:

- 5½-gallon glass carboy

- 3-foot length of 1- or 1½-inch plastic tubing (or as large as the inner diameter of the opening in the carboy will allow)

- Clean 1 gallon milk jug half-full of water

Cleaning the Carboy

Once you've racked your beer into the secondary fermenter, you will be faced with the task of cleaning your carboy. Fermentation leaves a thick sludge of spent yeast in the bottom of the fermenter. Pouring a gallon or so of warm water into the carboy and sloshing it around will help get rid of this. There will also be a ring of beer residue around the neck of the bottle. You can scrub this off with a bent bottle brush. Finally, invert the carboy over your bottle washer and blast out any remaining gunk. It's not a bad idea to then fill it with a PBW solution or a solution of baking soda and water and allow it to soak for a few days. Then you can empty it and rinse it out thoroughly to await the next batch.

Take care when emptying the carboy. A full carboy is heavy and fragile, and if it is wet it can really be a handful. As you pour, air is forced into the narrow neck of the bottle and water is forced out, and the carboy will glug and splash all over the place. To avoid this problem, take a racking cane, which is a long, rigid plastic tube used in siphoning, and place it in the carboy. Be sure to keep the end of the tube in the air bubble that forms as you pour. This will allow air to flow easily into the bottle, avoiding a potential mess.

The racking cane relieves air pressure inside the carboy, allowing easier pouring.

One-Gallon Batches

There are many good reasons for starting small when brewing. Experimenting with new ingredients or unfamiliar brewing styles, brewing test batches to perfect a recipe, or getting your feet wet as a new brewer before making a commitment to larger batches are all possibilities. Also the sheer bulk of fermenters, carboys, bottles, buckets, and sundry other equipment needed for home-scale brewing may be daunting to those with small living spaces.

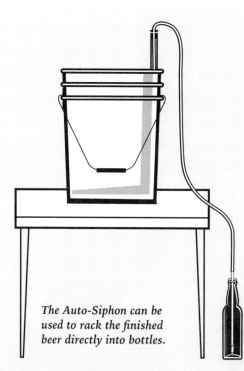

The Auto-Siphon can be used to rack the finished beer directly into bottles.

Bottling with the Auto-Siphon

The Auto-Siphon may be used in bottling, taking the place of the spigot in the standard bottling bucket. This means that any bucket can serve as a bottling bucket. Siphon the beer from the fermenter into a sanitized bucket and add your priming sugar solution. Now put the Auto-Siphon in the bucket and attach a filler wand to the end of the tubing. Remove the head of the wand so it doesn't blow off from air pressure, start the siphon, and then reattach the head and fill your bottles.

Small-batch brewing can be done with minimum equipment. A 2-gallon pot for a boiling kettle, a stirring spoon, a grain bag, a funnel with a mesh bottom to catch the hops, a 1-gallon glass jug, a stopper, a fermentation lock and a length of tubing, and a catch basin to make a blow-by system are all that you need. A gram scale to weigh the hops and malt grains is extremely useful but not vital unless you plan to make many small batches. To bottle the small batch you'll need a small Auto-Siphon or racking cane, plastic tubing, a capper, caps, and eight or so bottles. Carbonation drops (essentially small hard candies with just enough sugar to prime one bottle of beer) are the best option for priming a small batch. Muntons and Coopers both produce them, and they are available at any well-stocked homebrew store. Also bear in mind that sanitation is just as important on a small scale as it is on a larger scale.

Scaling down a recipe is a simple matter of using algebra (or plugging a few numbers into a brewing program such as BeerSmith). Multiply the amount of each ingredient in your recipe by the batch size, then divide by the original batch size. So if a 5-gallon batch of Diamond Jubilee ESB calls for 10 ounces of crystal malt, a 1-gallon batch would require 2 ounces [(1 × 10) ÷ 5 = 2].

The boil times are the same for small and large beer batches, although the time to reach boil temperatures will be much shorter. A cold-water bath can be very useful in bringing down the temperature of a hot brew pot.

Micro Mini Bitter

This tasty British ale is a miniaturized version of our Diamond Jubilee ESB on page 32. It's not aggressively hopped, and it serves as a good starting place for your own mini-batch experiments.

INITIAL GRAVITY: 1.033–1.040
FINAL GRAVITY: 1.012–1.015
YIELD: 1 GALLON

0.4 ounce (11.3 g) Chocolate malt

2 ounces (56 g) 60° Lovibond English Crystal malt

1 pound (454 g) dry extra light malt extract

0.3 ounce (8.5 g) Northern Brewer bittering hops (60-minute boil)

0.1 ounce (2.8 g) East Kent Goldings flavoring hops (15-minute boil)

0.1 ounce (2.8 g) Fuggles flavoring hops (15-minute boil)

0.1 ounce (2.8 g) Willamette aroma hops (added after boil)

1 packet Wyeast #10288 London Ale or Fermentis Safale S-04 ale yeast

6 carbonation drops for priming

3

INGREDIENTS AND RECIPE FORMULATION

The modern homebrewer has a global ingredients list. As the hobby has grown, so has the availability of new products from all over the world. There are so many choices in ingredients, equipment, and information now that we are almost awash in options. There are dozens of types of malt, scores of hop varieties, and a pharmacopoeia of yeast strains, and new ones are coming out all the time. If you can't find something locally, you can get it online, and usually pretty fast. On the other hand, working within restrictions can also be rewarding. Often we'll look in the supply cupboard and just modify an existing recipe or craft a new one to match what we have in stock, dropping by the brewstore to pick up whatever we lack. The point is that you don't have to feel limited by your recipe or the availability of ingredients. You can freely experiment, and this chapter will show you how.

Brewing ingredients break down into several types. These include: malt in some form or other, which provides the fermentable sugars; hops, which provide bitterness, flavor, and aroma, and also help preserve the beer; yeast, the tiny organisms that eat the malt sugars and produce alcohol and carbon dioxide (among other compounds); water; and adjuncts, which are just about anything else that you add to beer. Adjuncts are a very broad category that includes unmalted grains, nonmalt sugars, fruit, brewing herbs other than hops, and spices.

Other brewing ingredients include heading and clarifying agents, which are added to beer to produce a more lasting head of foam and to make a clearer beer, respectively.

Malt Extracts

Concentrated malt extracts are made by commercial maltsters. Most of the ones you find in homebrew shops are of European origin. There are several different kinds of malt extract available to the homebrewer. All are useful. Which kind you choose for a particular recipe depends on how you want the beer to turn out.

MALT EXTRACT SYRUP

Extract syrups come in cans, plastic bags, or plastic jugs. The syrup is the product of the mashing process, reduced in a vacuum until it contains about 20 percent water and 80 percent soluble solids. The syrup is a thick, molasses-like substance. When adding it to a brew pot, it is a good idea to take the pot off the heat to avoid burning the syrup.

Malt extract syrups come in barley or wheat forms and in light, amber, and dark colors, and may be hopped or unhopped.

Hopped malt extract is just extract syrup to which hops have been added in some form. Usually, hop extracts or oils are used instead of whole hops. The resulting syrup usually has good hop bitterness, but flavoring and aroma hops still need to be added to the recipe.

CAN KITS

Can kits are cans of malt extract that have been blended and hopped to produce a particular style of beer. The kit includes a packet of dried yeast under the cap, but it is a good idea to buy fresh yeast, since can kits don't get refrigerated in the brewstores. Can kits are intended to reduce brewing complexity to an absolute minimum. Whatever the directions say, it is always wise to boil the wort for at least 15 minutes and add some aroma hops after the boil. We recommend that you never add corn sugar to these kits; use malt extract instead. Kit instructions often suggest adding corn sugar, which will contribute a cidery flavor and thin body.

DRY MALT EXTRACT

If the maltster further reduces the amount of water in malt extract syrup, the result is dry malt extract, a sticky powder. Except for dry wheat malt extract, dry extracts are all essentially the same except for color. There may be some subtle differences between British and European dry malt extracts, but they're not significant. Dry malt extract comes in bulk, or packaged in preweighed plastic bags, in extra light, light, amber, and dark.

Lovibond

The color of the malt used in a recipe determines the color of the finished beer. One device for measuring the color of beer is the *Lovibond scale*. The higher the Lovibond number, the darker the malt or beer.

Malt Grains

Malt grains are sold by the pound in homebrew stores, in bulk or premeasured in sealed bags. Sometimes they are sold precrushed. There are many different kinds available to the homebrewer, each with different characteristics that will contribute unique qualities to your beer.

In the table of selected malt grains on pages 48–49, we provide information as to country of origin, degree Lovibond (a measurement of beer and grain color), description, and recommended amounts of each malt for a 5-gallon batch of beer.

Hops

Hops are the flowers of the female vine of *Humulus lupulus*. They are available loose, in plugs, and pelletized. (Hops are also available in the form of hop extracts and oils, but we won't be using them here.) Loose hops are whole hop flowers that come in 1-ounce bags. Hop plugs are whole hops that have been compressed into ½-ounce cakes that will loosen up in the boil. Pelletized hops have been ground and pressed into pellets. These are available in 1-ounce pouches. They take up less space per ounce than loose or plug hops, but they are also more difficult to remove from the wort.

HOPS AND THE BOIL

Hops contribute bitterness, flavor, and aroma to beer, depending on when they are added to the boil. Bitterness is derived from alpha acids, which require exposure to high heat and agitation before becoming soluble in wort. In other words, in order to release their bitterness, hops must be boiled for a relatively long time. Bittering hops are usually added early in the boil. Through the duration of the boil, the essential oils that provide flavoring and aroma are boiled off while the alpha acids undergo a process of isomerization (chemical transformation) that releases their bittering potential. This is the advantage of adding prehopped malt extract or can kits to homebrew. The downside of this, of course, is that the level of hoppiness is controlled by the malt manufacturer, not the homebrewer.

Hop flavor and aroma are derived from the hop essential oils. These oils are very delicate and volatile, and can be driven off by extended time in the wort boil. Flavoring hops are added during the later part of the boil to help retain as much flavor as possible. Some types of beer may use two or even three different varieties of flavoring hops. Aromatic or finishing hops are added immediately after the final boil, when the wort is still hot enough to sanitize the hops, and provide a delicately hoppy "nose." Adding hops during the secondary fermentation, known as dry hopping, can also impart a fresh hop aroma to the beer.

hop plug

loose hops

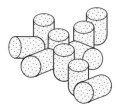

pelletized hops

A GUIDE TO MALT GRAINS

Malt Grain	Origin	Color	Comments
VIENNA MALT	Germany	4°L	Contributes caramel richness, malty flavor, and amber color. Mostly used in maltier lager styles. Use ¼ to 1 pound (113–454 g).
MUNICH MALT	Germany	5.7°L	Contributes malty flavor and orange color. Used in Belgian ales as well as dark and light lagers. Use ¼ to 1 pound (113–454 g).
BISCUIT MALT	Belgium	27°L	Adds a nutty, oatmeal biscuit flavor to beer. Used in milds, brown ales, and Belgian styles. Use ¼ to ¾ pound (113–340 g).
VICTORY MALT	United States	28°L	Adds toasted, nutty, biscuit, fresh bread flavors and deep gold to light brown color to beer. Especially good for brown ales. Use ¼ to ¾ pound (113–340 g).
SPECIAL ROAST MALT	United States	45°L	Adds body, roasted malt flavor, and deep orange color. Used in Belgian ales and some lagers. Use ¼ to ¾ pound (113–340 g).
CRYSTAL MALT/ CARAMEL MALT	United States, Germany, England	20–90°L	Usually British 2 row, 60°L. Contributes additional sweetness, body, and a golden or reddish color. Used in most styles of beer. Use ¼ to 1½ pounds (113–680 g).

Malt Grain	Origin	Color	Comments
CARAMEL 120 MALT	United States	120°L	Adds body, foam stability, deep red color, and a burnt sugar flavor. Used in amber ales, brown ales, and porters. Use ¼ to ¾ pound (113–340 g).
CHOCOLATE MALT	United States, England	400°L	Contributes a nutty, toasted flavor, and brown color. Used in British and Belgian ales, and porters. Use 2 ounces to ¾ pound (56–340 g).
ROASTED BARLEY	United States, England	500°L	Dark brown grain made from unmalted barley. Contributes roasted flavor, bitterness, and a brown head. A small amount adds a dark red color. Mainly used in stouts. Use 2 ounces to 1 pound (56–454 g).
BLACK PATENT MALT	England	530°L	Roasted malted barley that has had all its flavor driven off. Mostly used for coloring beer. Colors the beer's head and contributes a dry, burnt bitterness unlike that of hops. Used in porters and other black beers. Smoother flavor than roasted barley. Use 2 ounces to ¾ pound (56–340 g).
DEBITTERED BLACK MALT	Belgium	500–600°L	Black patent malt that has had its husk removed to eliminate its astringent qualities. Useful when dark color without bitterness is desired, such as in sweet stouts, schwarzbiers, and Black IPAs. Use 2 ounces to ¾ pound (56–340 g).

HOP VARIETIES

Different hops have different uses. Some are predominantly bittering, flavoring, or finishing hops, and some fulfill a combination of functions, depending on when and in what amount they are added to the wort. In recent years, the availability of certain hop varieties has varied wildly depending on weather and the hop market. Big and small brewers get first grabs on the hop harvest and leave the rest of us to scramble for what we can get. This has resulted in some shortages and some creative solutions, as hop blends are used to replace standard varieties. You can always make substitutions of similar hops to the ones your recipe calls for. Your local brewstore owner can be a lot of help in making suggestions for alternative hops. Don't get stuck on the specific hops in the recipe, but take them as a guide. A relaxed approach to this and other ingredients will make your brewing experience less stressful and more rewarding.

Alpha Acids

Alpha acids are the acids that form the main bittering agents in hops. The potential bitterness of hops is expressed in alpha acid units (AAUs), which is calculated as the percentage of alpha acids in the hops × the weight of the hops.

Low bitterness = 2 to 4% alpha acid content

Medium bitterness = 5 to 7% alpha acid content

High bitterness = 8 to 12% alpha acid content

Superhigh bitterness = 13 to 19% alpha acid content

A GUIDE TO HOP VARIETIES

The alpha acids give you an idea of the bitterness potential of each hop, with higher alpha values indicating greater bitterness.

Name	% Alpha Acids	Origin	Description and Uses
AMARILLO	5–10%	United States	Recommended for American ales. Citric, floral. Flavoring, aroma.
ATHANUM	7–10%	United States	Recommended for American ales. Citric, floral. Bittering, aroma.
CASCADE	5–7%	United States, Canada	Spicy floral aroma. Signature hop of American Pale Ales. Bittering, flavoring, aroma, dry hopping.
COLUMBUS	14–16%	United States	Good for American Pale Ales and IPAs. Citric, earthy with a clean bitterness. Bittering, aroma.
EAST KENT GOLDINGS	5–7%	England	Classic British ale hop. Delicate, subtly spicy. Bittering, flavoring, aroma, dry hopping.
FALCONER'S FLIGHT 7CS	9–11%	United States	Blend of hop varieties. Used in IPAs, American Pale Ales, and hoppy styles generally. Spicy, floral, earthy, fruity. Bittering, flavoring, aroma.
FUGGLES	4–7%	England, United States	Traditional British ale hop. Mild, earthy. Bittering, flavoring, aroma, dry hopping.
GALENA	12–14%	United States	Excellent high-alpha hop for American and English styles. Floral, citric. Bittering.
HALLERTAU	4–6%	Germany, United States	Traditional lager hop. Clean and floral. Bittering, flavoring, aroma.

(continued on next page)

(continued from previous page)

Name	% Alpha Acids	Origin	Description and Uses
NORTHERN BREWER	7.5–9.5%	Germany, United States, Belgium	Bold, bitter, aromatic. Bittering, aroma.
PERLE	6–9%	Germany, Czech Republic	For Continental and North American–style lagers. Spicy, floral. Bittering, aroma.
SAAZ	4–6%	Czech Republic	Traditional Pilsner hop. Floral, elegant. Bittering, flavoring, aroma, dry hopping.
SORACHI ACE	10–16%	New Zealand	Intensely lemony aroma. Bittering, flavoring, aroma, dry hopping.
STYRIAN GOLDINGS	5–7.5%	Slovenia	Excellent ale hop. Aromatic, clean. Bittering, flavoring, aroma, dry hopping.
SUMMIT	14–16%	United States	For blonde ales and light lagers. Funky, tangerine flavor. Bittering, flavoring, aroma.
TETTNANG	4–6%	Germany, United States	German and American lager hop. Spicy and distinctive. Bittering, flavoring, aroma.
WARRIOR	14–16%	United States	Use in any hoppy American style. Mild citrus, spicy. Bittering, aroma.
WILLAMETTE	5–7.5%	United States	Aromatic, developed as a slightly spicier American Fuggles. Bittering, flavoring, aroma, dry hopping.
ZYTHOS	10–12%	United States	Blend of several hop varieties. Designed for use in IPAs and hoppy American styles. Piney, citric, lemony, tangerine. Bittering, flavoring, aroma.

Yeast

After all of the necessary chemical reactions have taken place in the different stages of the boil, the wort is chilled and the critical component of yeast takes over to complete the transformation from ingredients to beer. Brewing yeast comes in two basic types: top-fermenting ale yeast and bottom-fermenting lager yeast.

TOP-FERMENTING AND BOTTOM-FERMENTING YEASTS

Top-fermenting yeasts are so called because they accumulate at the top of the fermenter. They favor warm temperatures, act rapidly, and tend to produce esters and other organic compounds that provide a variety of flavors. The use of top-fermenting yeast in ales accounts for their highly complex flavors.

Bottom-fermenting yeasts accumulate at the bottom of the fermenter. They act at lower temperatures than ale yeasts, and over a much longer period of time. This tends to produce a beer with more subtle flavor and little or no yeasty character.

Yeast is available as dried yeast, liquid yeast, and liquid yeast packs. Whatever form it's in, you need to keep it refrigerated until just before you're ready to brew.

Dried yeast comes in a packet just like bread yeast and is very easy to use. Unlike liquid yeast, it takes off rapidly (within a few hours) and finishes rapidly; there isn't a lot of waiting around.

Liquid yeast comes in a vial and can be used just as easily. Warm to room temperature and shake it up. It's a good idea to sanitize the outside of the vial and let it dry before pitching. Liquid yeast can be very active and foam dramatically when the vial is opened.

Liquid yeast packs (for example, Wyeast) contain a liquid yeast culture that is kept separate from a malt extract food source in a plastic bag. To use the yeast, you have to break the plastic bag inside the envelope, being careful not to break the envelope.

To break the bag, place the pack on a flat surface and give it a good whack with your hand. Wyeast packs have to work for 5 to 24 hours (older packs have to work longer) before you can add it to wort. Leave the pack undisturbed in a warm place. The yeast will begin to eat the malt extract in the pack, producing carbon dioxide, which will eventually cause the pack to swell up like a balloon. If the yeast pack isn't fully activated, it can still be used to ferment your beer. It will just take longer to begin working.

When ready to pitch, cut off one corner of the pack with a pair of sanitized scissors.

liquid yeast pack, a.k.a. yeast smack pack

Attenuation and Flocculation

ATTENUATION refers to the degree of fermentation produced by a yeast. Highly attenuative yeasts produce drier beers with slightly more alcohol; less attenuative yeasts produce maltier beers.

FLOCCULATION refers to the tendency of yeast to aggregate together in clumps and either rise to the top or sink to the bottom of the fermenter. Flocculant yeasts tend to be less attenuative, that is, they stop fermenting and drop out of solution earlier than less-flocculant yeasts.

A GUIDE TO YEAST VARIETIES

*Temperature ranges given are for optimal fermentation.

DRIED ALE YEAST Variety	Description*
FERMENTIS SAFALE S-04	Fast acting, reliable, mild-flavored yeast. Attenuation medium, flocculation high. Recommended for English-style ales. (65–70°F)
FERMENTIS SAFALE S-33	Reliable, consistent, clean-tasting yeast. Attenuation high, flocculation low. Recommended for English-style ales. (59–75°F)
FERMENTIS SAFALE US-05	Very reliable, mild-flavored yeast. Attenuation medium, flocculation low. Recommended for American-style ales. (59–75°F)
FERMENTIS SAFBREW T-58	Fast acting, spicy, phenolic. Attenuation high, flocculation high. Formulated for use in Belgian wit and lighter Belgian-style ales. (59–75°F)
MUNTONS MUNTONA ALE YEAST	Fast-acting yeast with some fruity esters. Attenuation medium, flocculation low. (65–70°F)
DANSTAR NOTTINGHAM ALE YEAST	Fast-acting, nutty-tasting yeast. Produces a dry, crisp ale. Attenuation high, flocculation high. (57–70°F)
DANSTAR WINDSOR ALE YEAST	Fast acting, with only moderate attenuation. Leaves full body. Good for stouts, porters, bitters. (65–70°F)

(continued on next page)

(continued from previous page)

DRIED LAGER YEAST

Variety	Description*
FERMENTIS SAFLAGER S-23 LAGER YEAST	Authentic German lager yeast. Produces dry, clean-tasting lagers. Best at low fermentation temperatures. Good flocculation, excellent attenuation. (50–57°F)
FERMENTIS SAFLAGER W-34/70 LAGER YEAST	Weihenstephan German lager yeast. Produces clean-tasting, malty lagers. Attenuation medium, flocculation high. (48–59°F)
BREWFERM LAGER YEAST	European-style lager yeast. Produces clean-tasting, malty lagers. Attenuation high, flocculation high. (50–59°F)

LIQUID ALE YEAST

Variety	Description*
WYEAST #1968 LONDON ESB	Malty, fruity. Attenuation medium, flocculation very high. Recommended for bitters, pale ales, and porters. (64–72°F)
WYEAST #1028 LONDON ALE	Bold, woody, slight diacetyl (butterscotch) touch. Attenuation medium, flocculation medium. Recommended for most British ales. (60–72°F)
WYEAST #1099 WHITBREAD ALE	Very reliable, fast-starting yeast blend. Has a unique flavor. Attenuation medium, flocculation high. (65–70°F)
WYEAST #3068 WEIHENSTEPHAN WEIZEN	Very reliable, clovelike. Attenuation medium, flocculation low. For Bavarian wheat beer. (64–75°F)

WYEAST 3787 TRAPPIST HIGH GRAVITY	Fruity, phenolic, alcohol-tolerant yeast. Attenuation medium, flocculation medium to low. Recommended for high-gravity Belgian ales. (64–78°F).
WHITE LABS WLP001 CALIFORNIA ALE	Clean and balanced. Attenuation medium to high, flocculation medium. Recommended for almost any style of ale. (64–72°F)
WHITE LABS WLP007 DRY ENGLISH ALE	Mild-flavored, fast-acting yeast. Attenuation high, flocculation high. Adaptable to both English- and American-style ales. Recommended for high-gravity beers such as Scottish Ales and barleywine-style ales. (65–70°F)
WHITE LABS WLP011 EUROPEAN ALE	Malty, clean flavored. Attenuation medium to low, flocculation medium. Recommended for altbier, Kölsch, English ales, and fruit beers. (65–70°F)
WHITE LABS WLP004 IRISH ALE	Mildly acidic with diacetyl (buttery) note. Recommended for use in stouts and porters. Attenuation medium, flocculation medium. (65–68°F)
WHITE LABS WLP500 TRAPPIST ALE	Fruity, phenolic, alcohol-tolerant yeast. Attenuation medium, flocculation medium to low. Recommended for high-gravity Belgian ales. (65–70°F)
WHITE LABS WLP351 BAVARIAN WEIZEN	Spicy, phenolic, clovelike. Attenuation medium, flocculation low. Produces classic Bavarian wheat beers. (66–70°F)

(continued on next page)

(continued from previous page)

LIQUID LAGER YEAST	
Variety	**Description***
WYEAST #2042 DANISH LAGER	Dry and crisp. Attenuation medium, flocculation low. Recommended for dry European-style lagers. (46–56°F)
WYEAST #2112 CALIFORNIA LAGER	Warm-fermenting lager yeast, prefers temperatures around 60°F. Attenuation medium, flocculation high. Recommended for use in California Common beers. (58–65°F)
WYEAST #2206 BAVARIAN LAGER	Rich, malty, and sweet. Attenuation medium, flocculation medium. Recommended for bocks, Vienna lagers, Märzens, and Oktoberfests. (46–56°F)
WHITE LABS WLP840 AMERICAN LAGER	Clean, dry, and fruity. High attenuation, medium flocculation. Recommended for American-style Pilsners. (50–55°F)
WHITE LABS WLP810 SAN FRANCISCO LAGER	Malty, woody, with some fruitiness. Attenuation medium, flocculation high. Can be fermented down to 50°F to produce Märzens, Pilsners, and other lager styles. Recommended for California Common beers. (58–65°F)

Finings

Finings are clarifying agents added to the wort during the boil or fermentation. They precipitate out proteins, yeast, and other solids from the wort, resulting in a clearer finished beer. The most commonly used finings are Irish moss and gelatin.

Irish moss is a dried, pulverized seaweed that is added during the boil to help coagulate proteins. It is much more effective if hydrated (soaked) overnight before brewing. Most of our recipes call for 1 teaspoon in 1 cup warm water. It's a good idea to add Irish moss to the boil, whether the recipe calls for it or not — unless you're brewing a weizen or a wit beer.

Plain, unflavored gelatin is added during secondary fermentation or at bottling as a fining agent. One-quarter ounce of gelatin added to 1 pint of water is sufficient for 5 gallons of beer. You can make this mixture at the same time that you boil your priming sugar solution. But don't boil the gelatin, or it will coagulate and fail to clear the beer. Gelatin produces very clear beer, and even makes pouring the beer easier, because it coagulates the sediments at the bottom of the bottle.

Recipe Formulation

Once you have been brewing for a while, you will probably want to start creating your own recipes. This is one of the most rewarding aspects of homebrewing and is not as difficult as it might sound. As you brew, you will soon get a feel for what characteristics different ingredients add to the finished product. You will develop preferences not only among beer styles, but also among types of hops, yeast, and malt extracts.

CHOOSING A STYLE

There is no end to the styles of beer you can brew, or the variations within each style. If you like a microbrewed or imported brew, why not try to replicate it in your own home brewery? You can also take advantage of the hundreds of different kinds of can kits available and experiment with modifying them according to certain beer styles.

Basing a recipe on a can kit is one way for beginning brewers to approach beer styles. Another method is to try to match your recipe to a style description. We've included a chart (shown at right) showing target specific gravity, alpha acid units, comments, and amounts of flavoring hops for each style. If you know the basic parameters for a style and the ingredients that go into it, there's no reason that you can't create recipes for that style.

SELECTING MALTS AND EXTRACTS

There are three things to consider when choosing malt extracts: *specific gravity, color,* and whether to use a *hopped or unhopped extract.* Specific gravity will tell you certain things about the finished beer, such as how much alcohol it will have and how malty it will be. Choosing a light, amber, or dark malt will determine what color the beer will be. Unless we're brewing a very basic beer, we like to use malt grains to color our beer (more on that shortly). If you use hopped malt extract (or even a can kit) in your recipe, you'll need to use less hops. If you use an unhopped extract, you'll need more hops, and you'll have to boil them longer.

The style chart on the next page will tell you roughly what the specific gravity of each style should be. A general rule of thumb is that 1 pound of malt extract syrup will yield

STYLE GUIDELINES FOR RECIPE FORMULATION

Style	Specific Gravity	AAU	Comments	Flavoring Hops
ALT	1.040–1.057	12–22	*Store cold*	no
BITTER	1.030–1.038	7–10	½ oz. aroma	1–2 oz.
BOCK	1.064–1.074	12–20	no aroma	½–1 oz.
BROWN ALE	1.040–1.055	8–12	½ oz. aroma	1–2 oz.
CALIFORNIA COMMON	1.047–1.052	12–15	*Ferment warm*	½ oz.
CREAM ALE	1.042–1.048	7–9	*Store cold*	no
CZECH PILSNER	1.045–1.052	10–14	½ oz. aroma	½–1 oz.
DUBBEL	1.040–1.080	7–8	½ oz. aroma	1 oz.
DUNKEL	1.045–1.058	12–15	¼ oz. aroma	1–2 oz.
ESB	1.046–1.060	9–11	½–1 oz. aroma	1–2 oz.
GERMAN PILSNER	1.040–1.050	12–16	½ oz. aroma	½–2 oz.
INDIA PALE	1.050–1.070	14–18	1 oz. dry hop	1–2 oz.
MÄRZEN	1.050–1.065	12–15	½ oz. aroma	½–2 oz.
MILD	1.030–1.040	6–8	½–2 oz. aroma	no
OLD	1.052–1.080	15–17	½ oz. aroma	no
PALE ALE	1.042–1.060	12–14	1 oz. dry hop	1–2 oz.
PORTER	1.040–1.060	9–11	½–1 oz. aroma	no
SCOTCH ALE	1.040–1.050	7–8	low carbonation	no
STOUT, DRY	1.035–1.050	12–15	roasted barley	no
STOUT, SWEET	1.035–1.060	9–12	*Add lactose*	no
TRIPEL	1.065–1.089	5–7	½ oz. dry hop	1 oz.
WEIZEN	1.040–1.055	4–6	40–60% wheat malt	no

6 to 7 points of specific initial gravity. One pound of dry malt extract will give you 8 to 9 points of specific initial gravity. (A point of specific gravity is equal to 0.001 added to the specific gravity of water, which is 1.000; thus, 1 pound of dry malt extract will yield a specific initial gravity of 1.008 to 1.009.) However, calculating specific gravity is an exact science, and if you want to know precisely what each ingredient contributes to your beer, tools such as BeerSmith can help. There are also wort gravity and hop utilization calculating apps available online.

Almost all beer styles benefit from the addition of malt grains. Grains contribute many subtle characteristics that are missing from malt extract alone. The amount and type used will depend on the characteristics you are trying to extract from the grain. In the case of very dark beers such as stout, ⅛ to ½ pound of black patent malt will give your beer better color than will dark malt extract alone. A mix of Belgian malts or different crystal malts can lend the beer a rainbow of colors from amber to garnet. Crystal malt will add sweetness and depth to the body of a beer, while pale malt can lend a fresh grain flavor that is often lacking in extracts. The list of grains on pages 48–49 gives suggestions for amounts and styles.

SELECTING HOPS

The first thing to consider when choosing hops is bitterness. The second is the characteristics contributed by the hop variety you've chosen, and whether that character is suitable for the style of beer you want to brew. Once you've determined these things, picking the hops should be a simple matter of deciding which varieties to use.

In the style chart (page 61), we use alpha acid units (AAUs) to describe bitterness. AAU is a measure of the bitterness potential of hops for a given volume of beer. AAU is determined by multiplying the percentage of alpha acids in a given hop variety by the number of ounces used. For instance, 2 ounces of Cascade hops (5 to 7 percent alpha acid) would give 10 to 14 AAU: (5 to 7) × 2 = (10 to 14). Match the AAU given in the style chart to the AAU value of the hops you plan to use.

Flavoring is a bit less scientific. We've given rough estimates for flavoring hops in the style chart. One of the factors that distinguishes recipes and styles from each other is the variety and amounts of flavoring hops they use, as well as the time they spend in the boil. This is an area where homebrewers experiment according to their individual tastes. Hoppy styles such as India Pale Ale (IPA) could easily take more flavor or bitterness than we've indicated. Consult the hop varieties chart (pages 51–52) for suggestions on which hops to use in different beer styles.

Aroma and dry hops also shouldn't be overlooked when designing beer recipes. We make suggestions about the amount of aromatic and dry hops to use, but it's really up to you, the individual homebrewer. The freshest and most aromatic hops you can find are the best for aroma and dry hopping. Remember that a large part of your sense of taste is actually that of smell: good beer aroma equals better beer taste.

SELECTING YEAST

Usually, the first decision you will make is whether to brew a lager or an ale. That will determine what type of yeasts you will choose from. The next step is to choose between dry and liquid yeast. Most beginning homebrewers use dry yeast, although liquid yeast that is started correctly will generally start fermenting faster.

When you graduate to more advanced brewing, you'll want to take advantage of the many varieties of liquid yeast. If you want to brew Belgian, London, English, Irish, American, or Canadian ales, specific liquid yeasts are available. So are Danish, Munich, Pilsner, American, and Bavarian lager yeasts. Depending on what style of beer you want to brew, the choices can be many. Some styles of beer, however, such as weizen and California Common, make more exacting demands for specific yeast characteristics, limiting the number of choices.

Some brewers prefer to select yeast based on its behavior, rather than its country of origin or recommended style. A clean, neutral-tasting California ale strain used to ferment a bitter will let the hops shine through more than the estery traditional ale yeasts do. Similarly, using a malty Bavarian lager yeast in a typically dry Pilsner will leave a bit more residual smoothness. Homebrewers can use as much creativity with yeast selection as with any other aspect of the hobby.

Estimating Fermentables

A simple formula, based on the target specific initial gravity, can be used to estimate the amount (in pounds) of fermentables you need to include in your recipe: Divide the last 2 digits of the initial gravity by 10.

In the case of our Tripel, 89 ÷ 10 = 8.9 pounds of fermentables.

ADJUSTING WATER CHEMISTRY

The best water for homebrewing is pure and relatively free of chemicals such as chlorine. If your tap water tastes good and smells good, then it is probably fine to use for extract brewing. It's really only when you get into all-grain brewing that water quality becomes crucial. We use well water in our brewing and our "house flavor" has some metallic notes. These are probably due to minerals in the water, but since we don't mind them, we don't bother filtering them out.

In a lot of places the water supply is treated. Chlorine can be removed by allowing your brewing water to sit overnight, or by boiling. Chloramine, on the other hand, has to be removed with a charcoal filter, or you can use Campden tablets. Contact your municipality to find out which chemical they are using.

As a general rule, British ales are brewed using hard (mineralized) water and European lagers are brewed with soft water. Remember that hard water is better for extracting hop alpha acids than soft. If your water is soft, it's easy to harden it using Burton water salts or gypsum, available at your home-brew store. Add between 1 and 2 teaspoons to the brewing water before the grains are steeped. If you desire softer water than your tap water, substitute half bottled water.

As a last resort you can buy bottled water for the whole batch. Many bottled waters are less suitable for brewing than is tap water because some minerals essential for brewing have been distilled or filtered out. Again, you can harden the bottled water with Burton water salts.

Recipe Design: A Crash Course

The best way to teach recipe design is to show you how we do it with an example. We'll start with a Belgian Tripel, a malty, strong ale.

Consulting the style chart, we find that the target initial gravity should be between 1.065 and 1.089, or roughly 9 pounds of fermentables (ingredients containing sugar to be fermented). In our Belgian Tripel we use honey, so we'll add 3 pounds of honey to 6.6 pounds of Northwest gold extract syrup. (Any brand of malt extract would do — Northwest is a favorite because it's fairly inexpensive and generally of good quality.)

Now we'll pick malt grains. We note from the chart on page 48 that Vienna malt and Munich malt add interesting characters and aren't too dark for Tripel. We'll add ½ pound of each. Looking at the style guidelines chart on page 61, Tripel has 5 to 7 AAUs. Adding 1 ounce of Styrian Goldings hops will give exactly the right bitterness (5 to 7 percent alpha acids × 1 ounce = 5 to 7 AAU). We'll add ½ ounce of Saaz hops for dry hopping.

That leaves the yeast. Tripel is a high-gravity, malty style with strong, characteristic esters. An alcohol-tolerant Belgian strain such as Trappist Ale would work best. Both Wyeast and White Labs offer it in liquid form. Belgian yeasts are, however, wildly variant, and you may want to seek out more yeasts and repeat batches with different strains.

RECIPES AND STYLES

The following recipes are a selection of the many we have developed in our years of homebrewing. They've all been formulated to be easy to brew and tasty to drink. In most cases we've included a very simple and then a slightly more complicated version of each beer, so that you can get a feel for the style before attempting something a little more challenging.

We encourage you to experiment with these recipes. Adding a little more grain, or a different strain of hops, can have a significant effect on the flavor, color, and aroma of the finished beer. Many homebrewers use an experimental approach to brewing, changing the recipes slightly each time they brew, and letting their taste buds guide them.

Three of these recipes, Juniper-Ginger Pale Ale, Penobscot Smoked Porter, and Bonton Ferry Black IPA, were contributed fresh for this edition by the good people at our local brewstore, Central Street Farmhouse in Bangor, Maine. These and many other tested recipes are also available as kits.

California Common is one of the few styles originating in America. It's a smooth, well-hopped beverage fermented with lager yeasts at ale temperatures.

Demologos Common Beer

INITIAL GRAVITY: 1.044–1.049
FINAL GRAVITY: 1.011–1.016

- 4 pounds (1.8 kg) Ironmaster Imperial Pale Ale kit
- 2 pounds (907 g) light dry malt extract
- ½ ounce (14 g) Cascade flavoring hops
- ½ ounce (14 g) Willamette aroma hops
- 1 vial White Labs WLP810 San Francisco Lager yeast
- ¾ cup (180 ml) corn sugar for priming

1. Heat 1½ gallons (5.7 L) cold water enough to melt malt extracts (100–120°F/38–49°C). Add the extracts and bring to a boil. Boil for 30 minutes.

2. Add the flavoring hops and boil for 15 minutes. Add the aroma hops. Allow to steep for 5 minutes.

3. Strain the hot wort into a fermenter containing 1½ gallons (5.7 L) of cold water. Rinse the hops with ½ gallon (1.9 L) 180°F (82°C) water. Top off up to 5 gallons (19 L).

4. Pitch the yeast when cool.

5. Ferment at ale temperatures (60–72°F/ 15.5–22°C). Prime and bottle when fermentation stops (2 to 3 weeks). Age for 4 to 6 weeks at cellar temperature (55°F/13°C) before drinking.

Rogue Torpedo Common Beer

INITIAL GRAVITY: 1.045–1.050
FINAL GRAVITY: 1.012–1.015

- ½ pound (227 g) Vienna malt
- 6.6 pounds (3 kg) amber malt extract syrup
- 2 ounces (56 g) Northern Brewer bittering hops
- ½ ounce (14 g) Cascade flavoring hops
- ½ ounce (14 g) Cascade aroma hops
- 1 packet Wyeast #2112 California Lager yeast
- ½ ounce (14 g) Willamette dry hops
- ¾ cup (180 ml) corn sugar for priming

1. Heat 1½ gallons (5.7 L) cold water to 165°F (74°C). Put the crushed grains in a grain bag and immerse in the hot water. Steep for 15 minutes, in water between 150°F and 170°F (65.5–77°C). Remove the grains and rinse over the brew pot with ½ gallon (1.9 L) 180°F (82°C) water.

2. Add the extract and the bittering hops. Boil for 45 minutes. Add the flavoring hops and boil for 15 minutes longer. Turn off heat and add the aroma hops. Steep for 5 minutes.

3. Strain the hot wort into a fermenter containing 1½ gallons (5.7 L) cold water. Rinse the hops with ½ gallon (1.9 L) 180°F (82°C) water. Top off up to 5 gallons (19 L).

4. Pitch the yeast when cool.

5. Ferment at ale temperatures (60–72°F/15.5–22°C). When fermentation dies down, add the dry hops. Prime and bottle when fermentation stops (2 to 3 weeks). Age for 4 to 6 weeks at cellar temperature (55°F/13°C) before drinking.

Bitter is cask-carbonated, dry, mildly hopped, and brewed from low gravities (and is therefore low in alcohol).

Elephant & Castle Bitter

INITIAL GRAVITY: 1.045–1.056
FINAL GRAVITY: 1.014–1.018

3¾ pounds (1.7 kg) Coopers Bitter kit

2 pounds (907 g) light dry malt extract

1 ounce (28 g) East Kent Goldings flavoring hops

½ ounce (14 g) Willamette aroma hops

1 packet Danstar Windsor Ale yeast

⅔ cup (160 ml) corn sugar for priming

1. Heat 1½ gallons (5.7 L) cold water enough to melt malt extracts (100–120°F/38–49°C). Add the extracts and bring to a boil. Boil for 30 minutes.

2. Add the flavoring hops and boil for 15 minutes. Remove from heat and add the aroma hops. Allow to steep for 5 minutes.

3. Strain the hot wort into a fermenter containing 1½ gallons (5.7 L) cold water. Rinse the hops with ½ gallon (1.9 L) 180°F (82°C) water. Top off up to 5 gallons (19 L).

4. Pitch the yeast when cool.

5. Ferment at ale temperatures (60–72°F/15.5–22°C). Prime and bottle when fermentation stops (7 to 10 days). Age for 2 weeks at cellar temperature (55°F/13°C) before drinking.

Brown ale is a mild, nutty, lightly hopped, and fairly low-alcohol beer.

Flying Finster Brown Ale

INITIAL GRAVITY: 1.042–1.050
FINAL GRAVITY: 1.015–1.019

4 pounds (1.8 kg) Mountmellick Brown Ale kit

2 pounds (907 g) dark dry malt extract

½ ounce (14 g) East Kent Goldings flavoring hops

1 packet Fermentis Safale S-04 ale yeast

⅔ cup (160 ml) corn sugar for priming

1. Heat 1½ gallons (5.7 L) cold water enough to melt malt extracts (100–120°F/38–49°C). Add the extracts and bring to a boil. Boil for 30 minutes.

2. Add the flavoring hops and boil for 15 minutes. Turn off heat and allow to cool.

3. Strain the hot wort into a fermenter containing 1½ gallons (5.7 L) cold water. Rinse the hops with ½ gallon (1.9 L) 180°F (82°C) water. Top off up to 5 gallons (19 L).

4. Pitch the yeast when cool.

5. Ferment at ale temperatures (60–72°F/15.5–22°C). Prime and bottle when fermentation stops (7 to 10 days). Age for 2 weeks at cellar temperature (55°F/13°C) before drinking.

Ecce Thump Brown Ale

INITIAL GRAVITY: 1.040–1.058
FINAL GRAVITY: 1.015–1.020

- ⅛ pound (57 g) black patent malt

- ⅓ pound (151 g) biscuit malt

- ½ pound (227 g) 80° Lovibond English crystal malt

- 6.6 pounds (3 kg) light malt extract syrup

- 1½ ounces (42 g) East Kent Goldings bittering hops

- ½ ounce (14 g) Fuggles aroma hops

- 1 packet Wyeast #1968 London Ale yeast

- ⅔ cup (160 ml) corn sugar for priming

1. Heat 1½ gallons (5.7 L) cold water to 150°F (65.5°C). Put the crushed grains in a grain bag and immerse in the hot water. Allow to steep for 15 minutes, keeping the water temperature between 150°F and 170°F (65.5–77°C). Remove from heat. Remove the grain bag and rinse over the brew pot with ½ gallon (1.9 L) 180°F (82°C) water.

2. Add the extract and the bittering hops. Return to heat and boil for 45 minutes. Add the aroma hops. Allow to steep for 5 minutes.

3. Strain the hot wort into a fermenter containing 1½ gallons (5.7 L) cold water. Rinse the hops with ½ gallon (1.9 L) 180°F (82°C) water. Top off up to 5 gallons (19 L).

4. Pitch the yeast when cool.

5. Ferment at ale temperatures (60–72°F/15.5–22°C). Prime and bottle when fermentation stops (1 to 2 weeks). Age for 3 weeks at cellar temperature (55°F/13°C) before drinking.

Mild is light brown, very light-bodied, very lightly hopped, with a malty taste – as malty as possible given the very low starting gravity. It is a good thirst quencher.

Frantic Mild

INITIAL GRAVITY: 1.032–1.041
FINAL GRAVITY: 1.012–1.016

3.3 pounds (1.5 kg) amber malt extract syrup

2 pounds (907 g) dark dry malt extract

2 ounces (56 g) Fuggles bittering hops

½ ounce (14 g) East Kent Goldings aroma hops

2 packets Muntons Muntona ale yeast

⅔ cup (160 ml) corn sugar for priming

1. Heat 1½ gallons (5.7 L) cold water enough to melt malt extracts (100–120°F/38–49°C). Remove from heat and add the extracts and bittering hops.

2. Return to heat and boil for 60 minutes. Add the aroma hops. Turn off heat and allow to steep for 5 minutes.

3. Strain the hot wort into a fermenter containing 1½ gallons (5.7 L) cold water. Rinse the hops with ½ gallon (1.9 L) 180°F (82°C) water. Top off up to 5 gallons (19 L).

4. Pitch the yeast when cool.

5. Ferment at ale temperatures (60–72°F/15.5–22°C). Prime and bottle when fermentation stops (7 to 10 days). Age for 2 weeks at cellar temperature (55°F/13°C) before drinking.

Kew Gardens Mild

INITIAL GRAVITY: 1.036–1.043
FINAL GRAVITY: 1.014–1.018

⅛ pound (57 g) Munich malt

½ pound (227 g) 60° Lovibond crystal malt

3.3 pounds (1.5 kg) dark malt extract syrup

1½ pounds (680 g) amber dry malt extract

1½ ounces (42 g) Fuggles bittering hops

½ ounce (14 g) Fuggles aroma hops

1 packet Fermentis Safale S-33 ale yeast

⅔ cup (160 ml) corn sugar for priming

1. Heat 1½ gallons (5.7 L) cold water to about 150°F (65.5°C). Put the crushed grains in a grain bag and immerse in the hot water. Allow to steep for 15 minutes, keeping the water temperature between 150°F and 170°F (65.5–77°C). Remove from heat. Remove the grain bag and rinse over the brew pot with ½ gallon (1.9 L) 180°F (82°C) water.

2. Add the extracts and the bittering hops. Return to heat and boil for 45 minutes. Remove from heat and add the aroma hops. Allow to steep for 5 minutes.

3. Strain the hot wort into a fermenter containing 1½ gallons (5.7 L) cold water. Rinse the hops with ½ gallon (1.9 L) 180°F (82°C) water. Top off up to 5 gallons (19 L).

4. Pitch the yeast when cool.

5. Ferment at ale temperatures (60–72°F/15.5–22°C). Prime and bottle when fermentation stops (1 to 2 weeks). Age for 3 weeks at cellar temperature (55°F/13°C) before drinking.

Pale ale is an amber- to copper-colored, bitter, malty beer of medium body and alcoholic strength.

Pale Horse Pale Ale

INITIAL GRAVITY: 1.044–1.055
FINAL GRAVITY: 1.014–1.018

3.3 pounds (1.5 kg) Black Rock East India Pale Ale kit

3.3 pounds (1.5 kg) pale malt extract syrup

½ ounce (14 g) East Kent Goldings flavoring hops

½ ounce (14 g) Fuggles aroma hops

1 packet Fermentis Safale S-04 ale yeast

⅔ cup (160 ml) corn sugar for priming

1. Heat 1½ gallons (5.7 L) cold water enough to melt malt extracts (100–120°F/38–49°C). Add the extracts and bring to a boil. Boil for 45 minutes.

2. Add the flavoring hops and boil for 15 minutes. Remove from heat and add the aroma hops. Allow to steep for 5 minutes.

3. Strain the hot wort into a fermenter containing 1½ gallons (5.7 L) cold water. Rinse the hops with ½ gallon (1.9 L) 180°F (82°C) water. Top off up to 5 gallons (19 L).

4. Pitch the yeast when cool.

5. Ferment at ale temperatures (60–72°F/15.5–22°C). Prime and bottle when fermentation stops (7 to 10 days). Age for 2 weeks at cellar temperature (55°F/13°C) before drinking.

Beyond the Pale Ale

INITIAL GRAVITY: 1.044–1.055
FINAL GRAVITY: 1.012–1.018

- ½ pound (227 g) 60° Lovibond English crystal malt
- ¼ pound (113 g) toasted malt
- 4 pounds (1.8 kg) Ironmaster Imperial Pale Ale kit
- 2 pounds (907 g) amber dry malt extract
- 1 ounce (28 g) Galena bittering hops
- ½ ounce (14 g) East Kent Goldings flavoring hops
- ½ ounce (14 g) Willamette aroma hops
- 1 packet Fermentis Safale S-04 ale yeast
- ⅔ cup (160 ml) corn sugar for priming

1. Heat 1½ gallons (5.7 L) cold water to about 150°F (65.5°C). Put the crushed grains in a grain bag and immerse in the hot water. Allow to steep for 15 minutes, keeping the water temperature between 150°F and 170°F (65.5–77°C). Remove from heat. Remove the grain bag and rinse over the brew pot with ½ gallon (1.9 L) 180°F (82°C) water.

2. Add the extracts and the bittering hops. Return to heat and boil for 45 minutes. Add the flavoring hops. Boil for 15 minutes. Remove from heat and add the aroma hops. Allow to steep for 5 minutes.

3. Strain the hot wort into a fermenter containing 1½ gallons (5.7 L) cold water. Rinse the hops with ½ gallon (1.9 L) 180°F (82°C) water. Top off up to 5 gallons (19 L).

4. Pitch the yeast when cool.

5. Ferment at ale temperatures (60–72°F/15.5–22°C). Prime and bottle when fermentation stops (2 to 3 weeks). Age for 3 to 4 weeks at cellar temperature (55°F/13°C) before drinking.

Juniper-Ginger Pale Ale

INITIAL GRAVITY: 1.050–1.054
FINAL GRAVITY: 1.013–1.015

½ pound (227 g) Cara-Pils malt

¼ pound (113 g) Victory malt

6.6 pounds (3 kg) Briess Golden Light malt extract syrup

1 ounce (28 g) Tettnang bittering hops

1 ounce (28 g) Tettnang flavoring hops

½ ounce (14 g) ginger root

½ ounce (14 g) juniper berries

1 packet Fermentis Safale S-04 or 1 vial White Labs WLP002 English Ale yeast

¾ cup (180 ml) corn sugar for priming

1. Heat 1½ gallons (5.7 L) cold water to about 150°F (65.5°C). Put the crushed grains in a grain bag and immerse in the hot water. Allow to steep for 15 minutes, keeping the water temperature between 150°F and 170°F (65.5–77°C). Remove the grain bag and rinse over the brew pot with ½ gallon (1.9 L) 180°F (82°C) water.

2. Add the extract and the bittering hops. Boil for 30 minutes. Add the flavoring hops and boil for 15 minutes. Add the ginger root and juniper berries and boil for 15 minutes longer. Allow to steep until cool enough to handle.

3. Strain the hot wort into a fermenter containing 1½ gallons (5.7 L) cold water. Rinse the hops with ½ gallon (1.9 L) 180°F (82°C) water. Top off up to 5 gallons (19 L).

4. Pitch the yeast when cool.

5. Ferment at ale temperatures (60–72°F/15.5–22°C). Prime and bottle when fermentation stops (2 to 3 weeks). Age for 3 to 4 weeks at cellar temperature (55°F/13°C) before drinking.

India Pale Ale (IPA) is a bigger, bolder version of Pale Ale with more hops and higher alcohol content. Black IPAs are popular among homebrewers and microbrewers.

Bonton Ferry Black IPA

INITIAL GRAVITY: 1.049–1.057
FINAL GRAVITY: 1.013–1.016

½ pound (227 g) Special B malt

½ pound (227 g) debittered black malt

6.6 pounds (3 kg) Briess Sparkling Amber malt extract syrup

1 pound (454 g) Briess Golden Light malt extract

1 ounce (28 g) Columbus bittering hops

1 ounce (28 g) Cascade flavoring hops

1 ounce (28 g) Ahtanum dry hops

1 packet Fermentis Safale US-05 or White Labs WLP001 California Ale yeast

¾ cup (180 ml) corn sugar for priming

1. Heat 1½ gallons (5.7 L) cold water to 150°F (65.5°C). Put the crushed grains in a grain bag and immerse in the hot water. Allow to steep for 15 minutes, keeping the water temperature between 150°F and 170°F (65.5–77°C). Remove the grain bag and rinse over the brew pot with ½ gallon (1.9 L) 180°F (82°C) water.

2. Add the extracts and the bittering hops. Boil for 45 minutes. Add the flavoring hops and boil for 15 minutes longer. Allow to steep until the brew pot is cool enough to handle.

3. Strain the hot wort into a fermenter containing 1½ gallons (5.7 L) cold water. Rinse the hops with ½ gallon (1.9 L) 180°F (82°C) water. Top off up to 5 gallons (19 L).

4. Pitch the yeast when cool.

5. Ferment at ale temperatures (60–72°F/15.5–22°C). When fermentation slows, rack the beer to the secondary fermenter. Add the dry hops. Prime and bottle when fermentation stops (2 to 3 weeks). Age for 3 to 4 weeks.

Porter is a medium-bodied, moderately hopped dark ale of medium alcoholic strength.

Two Pints Off the Port Bow Porter

INITIAL GRAVITY: 1.044–1.052
FINAL GRAVITY: 1.014–1.019

3¾ pounds (1.7 kg) Coopers Dark Ale kit

3.3 pounds (1.5 kg) amber malt extract syrup

1 ounce (28 g) Willamette flavoring hops

1 packet Fermentis Safale S-04 ale yeast

½ cup (120 ml) corn sugar for priming

1. Heat 1½ gallons (5.7 L) cold water enough to melt malt extracts (100–120°F/38–49°C). Add the extracts and bring to a boil. Boil for 30 minutes.

2. Add the flavoring hops and boil for 15 minutes.

3. Strain the hot wort into a fermenter containing 1½ gallons (5.7 L) cold water. Rinse the hops with ½ gallon (1.9 L) 180°F (82°C) water. Top off up to 5 gallons (19 L).

4. Pitch the yeast when cool.

5. Ferment at ale temperatures (60–72°F/15.5–22°C). Prime and bottle when fermentation stops (7 to 10 days). Age for 2 weeks at cellar temperature (55°F/13°C) before drinking.

Dunderfunk Porter

INITIAL GRAVITY: 1.040–1.049
FINAL GRAVITY: 1.010–1.015

- ¼ pound (113 g) chocolate malt
- ¼ pound (113 g) roasted barley
- ½ pound (227 g) 60° Lovibond English crystal malt
- 4 pounds (1.8 kg) dark malt extract syrup
- 2½ pounds (1.1 kg) dark dry malt extract
- 1½ ounces (42 g) East Kent Goldings bittering hops
- ½ ounce (14 g) Willamette aroma hops
- 2 packets Muntons Muntona ale yeast
- ⅔ cup (160 ml) corn sugar for priming

1. Heat 1½ gallons (5.7 L) cold water to about 150°F (65.5°C). Put the crushed grains in a grain bag and immerse in the hot water. Allow to steep for 15 minutes, keeping the water temperature between 150°F and 170°F (65.5–77°C). Remove the grain bag and rinse over the brew pot with ½ gallon (1.9 L) 180°F (82°C) water.

2. Add the extracts and the bittering hops. Boil for 60 minutes. Remove from heat and add the aroma hops. Allow to steep for 5 minutes.

3. Strain the hot wort into a fermenter containing 1½ gallons (5.7 L) cold water. Rinse the hops with ½ gallon (1.9 L) 180°F (82°C) water. Top off up to 5 gallons (19 L).

4. Pitch the yeast when cool.

5. Ferment at ale temperatures (60–72°F/15.5–22°C). Prime and bottle when fermentation stops (2 to 3 weeks). Age for 3 to 4 weeks at cellar temperature (55°F/13°C) before drinking.

Penobscot Smoked Porter

INITIAL GRAVITY: 1.060–1.066
FINAL GRAVITY: 1.014–1.017

½ pound (227 g) flaked oats

¼ pound (113 g) smoked malt

½ pound (220g) Caramel 120 malt

¼ pound (113 g) Vienna malt

¼ pound (113 g) black patent malt

6.6 pounds (3 kg) Briess Sparkling Amber malt extract syrup

1 ounce (28 g) Columbus bittering hops

1 ounce (28 g) Brewer's Gold flavoring hops

1 packet Danstar Nottingham or 1 vial White Labs WLP011 European Ale yeast

⅔ cup (160 ml) corn sugar for priming

1. Heat 1½ gallons (5.7 L) cold water to 150°F (65.5°C). Put the crushed grains in a grain bag and immerse in the hot water. Allow to steep for 15 minutes, keeping the water temperature between 150°F and 170°F (65.5–77°C). Remove the grain bag and rinse over the brew pot with ½ gallon (1.9 L) 180°F (82°C) water.

2. Add the extract and the bittering hops. Boil for 45 minutes. Add the flavoring hops and boil for 15 minutes longer. Allow to steep until cool enough to handle.

3. Strain the hot wort into a fermenter containing 1½ gallons (5.7 L) cold water. Rinse the hops with boiled water. Top off up to 5 gallons (19 L).

4. Pitch the yeast when cool.

5. Ferment at ale temperatures (60–72°F/15.5–22°C). Prime and bottle when fermentation stops. Age for 4 to 6 weeks at cellar temperature (55°F/13°C) before drinking.

Stout is a black, bitter, and complex brew. Variations include dry, sweet, Imperial, and oatmeal stout. Stouts are fairly low in alcohol, with no hop flavor or aroma.

Susan's Sweet Stout

INITIAL GRAVITY: 1.050–1.055
FINAL GRAVITY: 1.016–1.019

3¾ pounds (1.7 kg) Black Rock Miner's Stout kit

2 pounds (907 g) dark dry malt extract

½ pound (227 g) dry wheat extract

1 ounce (28 g) Northern Brewer bittering hops

¼ pound (113 g) lactose

2 packets Muntons Muntona ale yeast

½ cup (120 ml) corn sugar or 1 cup (240 ml) dry malt extract for priming

1. Heat 1½ gallons (5.7 L) cold water enough to melt malt extracts (100–120°F/38–49°C). Add the extracts and bring to a boil.

2. Add the bittering hops. Boil for 60 minutes. Add the lactose for the final 15 minutes of boil.

3. Strain the hot wort into a fermenter containing 1½ gallons (5.7 L) cold water. Rinse the hops with ½ gallon (1.9 L) 180°F (82°C) water. Top off up to 5 gallons (19 L).

4. Pitch the yeast when cool.

5. Ferment at ale temperatures (60–72°F/15.5–22°C). Prime and bottle when fermentation stops (2 to 3 weeks), using corn sugar or malt extract for priming. Age for 3 weeks at cellar temperature (55°F/13°C) before drinking.

Finn McCool's Irish Stout

INITIAL GRAVITY: 1.045–1.064
FINAL GRAVITY: 1.012–1.016

- ½ pound (220 g) 60° Lovibond English crystal malt
- ½ pound (227 g) roasted barley
- 4 pounds (1.8 kg) Mountmellick Irish Stout kit
- 3 pounds (1.4 kg) dark malt extract syrup
- 1 ounce (28 g) Galena hop pellets
- 1 packet Fermentis Safale S-04 ale yeast
- ⅔ cup (160 ml) corn sugar for priming

1. Heat 1½ gallons (5.7 L) cold water to 150°F (65.5°C). Put the crushed grains in a grain bag and immerse in the hot water. Allow to steep for 15 minutes, keeping the water temperature between 150°F and 170°F (65.5–77°C). Remove from heat. Remove the grain bag and rinse over the brew pot with ½ gallon (1.9 L) 180°F (82°C) water.

2. Add the extracts and hops. Return to heat and boil for 60 minutes.

3. Strain the hot wort into a fermenter containing 1½ gallons (5.7 L) cold water. Rinse the hops with ½ gallon (1.9 L) 180°F (82°C) water. Top off up to 5 gallons (19 L).

4. Pitch the yeast when cool.

5. Ferment at ale temperatures (60–72°F/15.5–22°C). Prime and bottle when fermentation stops (2 to 3 weeks). Age for 3 to 4 weeks at cellar temperature (55°F/13°C) before drinking.

Weizen, or weiss, is a copper-colored, lightly hopped Bavarian wheat beer. Weizenbiers are spicy, cloudy, and slightly sour from the wheat and assertive yeast.

Stands to Weizen

INITIAL GRAVITY: 1.045–1.050
FINAL GRAVITY: 1.014–1.016

3.3 pounds (1.5 kg) wheat extract syrup

2 pounds (907 g) dry wheat malt extract

½ ounce (14 g) Hallertau bittering hops

1 packet Fermentis Safebrew WB-06 yeast

⅞ cup (210 ml) corn sugar for priming

1. Heat 1½ gallons (5.7 L) cold water enough to melt malt extracts (100–120°F/38–49°C). Add the extracts and bring to a boil.

2. Add the bittering hops. Boil for 60 minutes.

3. Strain the hot wort into a fermenter containing 1½ gallons (5.7 L) cold water. Rinse the hops with ½ gallon (1.9 L) 180°F (82°C) water. Top off up to 5 gallons (19 L).

4. Pitch the yeast when cool.

5. Ferment at ale temperatures (60–72°F/15.5–22°C). Prime and bottle when fermentation stops (1 to 2 weeks). Age for 3 weeks at cellar temperature (55°F/13°C) before drinking.

There's Always a Reason to Pour More Weizen

INITIAL GRAVITY: 1.059–1.063
FINAL GRAVITY: 1.016–1.019

½ pound (227 g) Special Roast malt

4 pounds (1.8 kg) Edme Superbrew Weizen kit

3.3 pounds (1.5 kg) wheat extract syrup

½ ounce (14 g) Tettnang bittering hops

1 vial White Labs WLP351 Bavarian Weizen yeast

⅞ cup (210 ml) corn sugar for priming

1. Heat 1½ gallons (5.7 L) cold water to about 150°F (65.5°C). Put the crushed grains in a grain bag and immerse in the hot water. Allow to steep for 15 minutes, keeping the water temperature between 150°F and 170°F (65.5–77°C). Remove the grain bag and rinse over the brew pot with ½ gallon (1.9 L) 180°F (82°C) water.

2. Add the extracts and return to a boil. Add the hops. Boil for 60 minutes.

3. Strain the hot wort into a fermenter containing 1½ gallons (5.9 L) cold water. Rinse the hops with ½ gallon (1.9 L) 180°F (82°C) water. Top off up to 5 gallons (19 L).

4. Pitch the yeast when cool.

5. Ferment at ale temperatures (60–72°F/15.5–22°C). Prime and bottle when fermentation stops (1 to 2 weeks). Age for 3 weeks at cellar temperature (55°F/13°C) before drinking.

About Lagers

In this basic brewing book, we've concentrated on ales because they are quick and easy to brew. Lagers are a little more complex. Lager yeasts are a different strain from ale yeasts and accumulate on the bottom of the fermenting vessel, rather than on top as with ales. Therefore, lagers are called "bottom-fermenting" beers, and ales are "top fermenting." Lagers require cooler temperatures than do ales, usually in the 40°F to 50°F range (60°F to 70°F is suitable for ales). For this reason, it's best to brew your lagers in fall or winter.

Lagers also require a secondary fermentation in a separate vessel. After primary fermentation is complete, and the bubbles in the airlock have slowed to once every 30 seconds, the beer is racked off into the secondary fermenter, usually a carboy. It is then left in a cold place to "lager" for several months. The resulting beer is very clear and clean tasting. Malt characteristics are quite evident in lagers.

Bock is a sweet, malty, full-bodied lager. There are many versions, including the more powerful doppelbock.

Headlock Bock

INITIAL GRAVITY: 1.060–1.065
FINAL GRAVITY: 1.011–1.014

⅛ pound (57 g) Munich malt

⅛ pound (57 g) 90° Lovibond German crystal malt

6 pounds (2.7 kg) dark malt extract syrup

2 ounces (56 g) Tettnang bittering hops

1 packet Fermentis Saflager W-34/70 lager yeast

½ cup (120 ml) corn sugar for priming

1. Heat 1½ gallons (5.7 L) cold water to 150°F (65.5°C). Put the crushed grains in a grain bag and immerse in the hot water. Allow to steep for 15 minutes, keeping the water temperature between 150°F and 170°F (65.5–77°C). Turn off heat. Remove the grain bag and rinse over the brew pot with ½ gallon (1.9 L) 180°F (82°C) water.

2. Add the extract and bring to a boil. Add the hops. Boil for 60 minutes.

3. Strain the hot wort into a fermenter containing 1½ gallons (5.7 L) cold water. Rinse the hops with ½ gallon (1.9 L) 180°F (82°C) water. Top off up to 5 gallons (19 L).

4. Pitch the yeast when cool.

5. Ferment at lager temperatures (45–55°F/ 7–13°C). Prime and bottle when fermentation stops (6 to 8 weeks). Age for 6 to 8 weeks at lager temperatures before drinking.

Doppelbock is a maltier, stronger version of bock, brewed from a higher original gravity than bock. It is a heavy beverage with a strong alcohol character.

Monitor Doppelbock

INITIAL GRAVITY: 1.074–1.080
FINAL GRAVITY: 1.015–1.019

7.5 pounds (3.4 kg) Black Rock Bock kit

2 pounds (907 g) Dutch light dry malt extract

1 ounce (28 g) Tettnang hops

1 packet Fermentis Saflager W-34/70 lager yeast

½ cup (120 ml) corn sugar for priming

1. Heat 1½ gallons (5.7 L) cold water enough to melt malt extracts (100–120°F/38–49°C).

2. Add the extracts and bring to a boil. Add the hops and boil for 60 minutes.

3. Strain the hot wort into a fermenter containing 1½ gallons (5.7 L) cold water. Rinse the hops with ½ gallon (1.9 L) 180°F (82°C) water. Top off up to 5 gallons (19 L).

4. Pitch the yeast when cool.

5. Ferment at lager temperatures (45–55°F/7–13°C). Prime and bottle when fermentation stops (6 to 8 weeks). Age for 1 to 4 months at lager temperatures before drinking.

German Pilsner is light-bodied, pale, dry, and assertively hopped.

Graf Zeppelin Pils

INITIAL GRAVITY: 1.040–1.045
FINAL GRAVITY: 1.010–1.015

3.3 pounds (1.5 kg) Brewferm Pilsner kit

2 pounds (907 g) Dutch extra light malt extract

1 ounce (28 g) Hallertau flavoring hops

½ ounce (14 g) Saaz aroma hops

1 packet Fermentis Saflager S-23 lager yeast

¾ cup (180 ml) corn sugar for priming

1. Heat 1½ gallons (5.7 L) cold water enough to melt malt extracts (100–120°F/38–49°C). Add the extracts and bring to a boil. Boil for 30 minutes.

2. Add the flavoring hops and boil for 15 minutes. Remove from heat, add the aroma hops, and allow to steep for 5 minutes.

3. Strain the hot wort into a fermenter containing 1½ gallons (5.7 L) cold water. Rinse the hops with ½ gallon (1.9 L) 180°F (82°C) water. Top off up to 5 gallons (19 L).

4. Pitch the yeast when cool.

5. Ferment at lager temperatures (45–55°F/7–13°C). Prime and bottle when fermentation stops (6 to 8 weeks). Age for 1 to 4 months at lager temperatures before drinking.

Tiny Ragged Pils

INITIAL GRAVITY: 1.048–1.052
FINAL GRAVITY: 1.014–1.018

½ pound (227 g) Vienna malt

3.3 pounds (1.5 kg) light unhopped malt extract syrup

2 pounds (907 g) Dutch extra light malt extract

1½ ounces (42 g) Hallertau bittering hops

½ ounce (14 g) Tettnang flavoring hops

½ ounce (14 g) Hallertau aroma hops

1 packet Wyeast 1007 German lager yeast

¾ cup (180 ml) corn sugar for priming

1. Heat 1½ gallons (5.7 L) cold water to 150°F (65.5°C). Put the crushed grains in a grain bag and immerse in the hot water. Allow to steep for 15 minutes, keeping the water temperature between 150°F and 170°F (65.5–77°C). Turn off heat. Remove the grain bag and rinse over the brew pot with ½ gallon (1.9 L) boiled water. Add the extracts and bring to a boil.

2. Add the bittering hops and boil for 60 minutes. Add the flavoring hops in the last 15 minutes of boil. Add the aroma hops, and allow to steep for 5 minutes.

3. Strain the hot wort into a fermenter containing 1½ gallons (5.7 L) cold water. Rinse the hops with ½ gallon (1.9 L) 180°F (82°C) water. Top off up to 5 gallons (19 L).

4. Pitch the yeast when cool.

5. Ferment at lager temperatures (45–55°F/7–13°C). Prime and bottle when fermentation stops (6 to 8 weeks). Age for 1 to 4 months at lager temperatures before drinking.

Dubbel and Tripel are two of the Belgian Trappist ales produced by monks living in this beer-intensive region.

Bishop's Ruin Dubbel

INITIAL GRAVITY: 1.070–1.076
FINAL GRAVITY: 1.014–1.017

3.3 pounds (1.5 kg) Brewferm Abbey kit

4 pounds (1.8 kg) light malt extract syrup

½ pound (227 g) brown sugar

1 teaspoon (5 g) Irish moss

1 ounce (28 g) Styrian Goldings flavoring hops

1 ounce (28 g) Saaz hop plugs for aroma

1 packet Fermentis Safebrew T-58 ale yeast

¾ cup (180 ml) corn sugar for priming

1. Heat 1½ gallons (5.7 L) cold water enough to melt malt extracts (100–120°F/38–49°C). Add the extracts, brown sugar, and Irish moss. Return to heat and boil for 60 minutes.

2. Add the flavoring hops in the last 10 minutes of boil. Remove from heat, add the hop plugs, and allow to steep for 5 minutes.

3. Strain the hot wort into a fermenter containing 1½ gallons (5.7 L) cold water. Rinse the hops with ½ gallon (1.9 L) 180°F (82°C) water. Top off up to 5 gallons (19 L).

4. Pitch the yeast when cool.

5. Ferment at ale temperatures (60–72°F/15.5–22°C). Prime and bottle when fermentation stops (3 to 6 weeks). Age for 6 weeks at cellar temperature (55°F/13°C) before drinking.

Tripel is fruity, estery, and strongly alcoholic. It ages well and continues to develop in the bottle.

Rose Window Tripel

INITIAL GRAVITY: 1.076-1.080
FINAL GRAVITY: 1.016-1.018

- ½ pound (227 g) British crystal malt

- ½ pound (227 g) Cara Munich malt

- ¼ pound (113 g) Cara Vienna malt

- 6 pounds (2.7 kg) light malt extract syrup

- 3 pounds (1.4 kg) honey

- 1 ounce (28 g) Styrian Goldings flavoring hops

- 1 vial White Labs WLP500 Trappist Ale yeast

- ½ ounce (14 g) Saaz dry hops

- ¾ cup (180 ml) corn sugar for priming

1. Heat 1½ gallons (5.7 L) cold water to about 150°F (65.5°C). Put the crushed grains in a grain bag and immerse in the hot water. Allow to steep for 15 minutes, keeping the water temperature between 150°F and 170°F (65.5–77°C). Turn off heat. Remove the grain bag and rinse over the brew pot with ½ gallon (1.9 L) 180°F (82°C) water.

2. Add the extract, honey, and flavoring hops. Boil for 45 minutes.

3. Strain the hot wort into a fermenter containing 1½ gallons (5.7 L) cold water. Rinse the hops with ½ gallon (1.9 L) 180°F (82°C) water. Top off up to 5 gallons (19 L).

4. Pitch the yeast when cool.

5. Ferment at ale temperatures (60–72°F/15.5–22°C). When fermentation begins to die down, add the dry hops to the fermenter. Prime and bottle when fermentation stops (3 to 6 weeks). Age for 6 to 8 weeks at cellar temperature (55°F/13°C) before drinking.

Duvel (Belgian for "devil") could fairly be described as a "stealth" ale; it looks, smells, and tastes like a Pilsner, but it's much stronger. Imbibe with care.

Beelzebub Duvel

INITIAL GRAVITY: 1.080–1.084
FINAL GRAVITY: 1.012–1.016

½ pound (227 g) Vienna malt

6.6 pounds (3 kg) Brewferm
    Diabolo extract kit (2 cans)

2 pounds (907 g) orange
    blossom honey

½ ounce (14 g) Saaz hop plugs

1 packet Fermentis Safebrew
    T-58 ale yeast

⅔ cup (160 ml) corn sugar for
    priming

1. Heat 1½ gallons (5.7 L) cold water to about 150°F (65.5°C). Put the crushed grains in a grain bag and immerse in the hot water. Allow to steep for 15 minutes, keeping the water temperature between 150°F and 170°F (65.5–77°C). Turn off heat. Remove the grain bag and rinse over the brew pot with ½ gallon (1.9 L) 180°F (82°C) water.

2. Add the extract and honey and boil for 60 minutes. Remove from heat and add the hop plugs. Allow to steep for 5 minutes.

3. Strain the hot wort into a fermenter containing 1½ gallons (5.7 L) cold water. Rinse the hops with ½ gallon (1.9 L) 180°F (82°C) water. Top off up to 5 gallons (19 L).

4. Pitch the yeast when cool.

5. Ferment at ale temperatures (60–72°F/15.5–22°C). Prime and bottle when fermentation stops (3 to 6 weeks). Age for 6 weeks at cellar temperature (55°F/13°C) before drinking.

GLOSSARY

ALE. Style of beer produced by top-fermenting yeast strains at relatively warm temperatures. Includes bitter, stout, porter, India Pale, and others.

ALPHA ACIDS. The acids that form the main bittering agents in hops.

BARLEY. A cereal grain, the seeds of which (barleycorns) are used in making beer. There are different varieties, 2-row and 6-row, which have different characteristics.

CARBOY. A clear plastic or glass bottle that can be used as a fermenting vessel.

COLD BREAK. The stage during the cooling of hot wort when proteins precipitate as suspended particles.

CONDITIONING. The stage during beer aging when carbonation develops.

ESTERS. Organic compounds that often have strong, fruity aromas.

FERMENTATION. The stage of the yeast's life cycle during which it eats and produces alcohol, carbon dioxide, and some flavors of beer.

FERMENTATION LOCK. A device that vents carbon dioxide from a vessel while keeping air out, preventing contamination.

FINING AGENT. An ingredient used to clarify beer, such as gelatin, Irish moss, and isinglass.

FINISHING HOPS. Hops added after the boil that contribute delicate aromas to the beer.

HYDROMETER. A graduated glass instrument used to measure the specific gravity of liquids such as unfermented wort and finished beer.

ISOMERIZATION. The process in which the arrangement of atoms in a compound are altered by heating or other means. During boiling, alpha acids in hops are isomerized and these isomers (iso-alpha acids) bitter the finished beer.

KRAUSEN. The large head of foam that forms on the surface of the wort during the early stages of fermentation.

LAGER. Style of beer produced by bottom-fermenting yeasts at low temperatures. Originated in Germany. Includes Märzens,

Pilsners, bocks, and Oktoberfests, among others.

MALT. Cereal grain (generally barley, but not always) that has been partially germinated, dried, or possibly roasted to produce different brewing characteristics.

MALT EXTRACT. Concentrated wort in syrup or powder form. Can be hopped or unhopped.

MASHING. The process of extracting sweet liquor from malted grains by means of temperature-controlled steeping.

PITCHING. Adding yeast to wort to begin the fermentation process.

PRIMARY FERMENTATION. The very active first phase of fermentation that proceeds from the time of pitching until the krausen drops.

PRIMARY FERMENTER. Vessel in which primary fermentation takes place. Can be either a plastic bucket or a carboy.

PRIMING. The process of adding sugar or malt extract to beer at bottling time to induce carbonation.

RACKING. The process of siphoning unfinished homebrew from the primary fermentation vessel to the secondary fermentation vessel or bottling bucket.

SECONDARY FERMENTATION. The less active, later stage of fermentation that proceeds from the time the krausen subsides until the yeast drops out of the solution.

SECONDARY FERMENTER. Vessel in which secondary fermentation takes place. Can be a carboy or plastic bucket.

SPARGING. The process of rinsing residual sugars from mashed grains with boiled water.

SPECIFIC GRAVITY. The weight of a liquid compared with an equal amount of pure water.

WORT. The unfermented solution of malt sugars, proteins, and other substances. Once fermentation is complete, it is called "beer."

YEAST. Microscopic organisms that produce the alcohol, carbon dioxide, and some of the flavors of beer through their life cycle.

APPENDIX A

Amounts and Conversions

LIQUID MEASURES

1 US gallon = 3.785 liters

1 US gallon = 0.833 Imperial gallons

1 Imperial gallon = 1.2 US gallons

1 Imperial pint = 20 ounces

1 US pint = 2 cups = 473 milliliters

DRY MEASURES

¼ pound = 113 grams

½ pound = 227 grams

¾ pound = 340 grams

1 pound = 454 grams

1½ pounds = 680 grams

1¾ pounds = 794 grams

2 pounds = 907 grams

3.3 pounds = 1.5 kilograms

3¾ pounds = 1.7 kilograms

TEMPERATURE

Degrees Celsius = ⅝ × (F − 32)

Degrees Fahrenheit = (⅗ × C) + 32

APPENDIX B

How to Use the Hydrometer

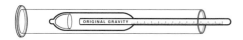

The hydrometer is a graduated glass instrument that measures the density or specific gravity of liquids. It is ordinarily used twice in basic brewing: first to test the specific gravity of the unfermented wort, and second to find the gravity of the finished beer. The initial reading is taken after the wort has been topped off up to 5 gallons but before the yeast is pitched, and it gives the brewer an idea of the amount of fermentables in the wort (original gravity). The second reading is used to confirm that fermentation is complete (final gravity). If your recipe is provided with initial and final gravity readings and you have followed it exactly, then your readings should fall within the range given. Yeast converts sugars in the fermentables into alcohol and carbon dioxide, so your final reading will always be less than your initial reading. A hydrometer reading that is higher than it ought to be may indicate that fermentation is not complete.

To take a reading, fill the plastic hydrometer container case with wort to about ½ inch from the top. Place the hydrometer in the wort and gently spin it with your fingers to remove air bubbles. Find where the liquid crosses the scale in the neck of the hydrometer. Write down this figure. When reading a hydrometer, you should sight directly across the top of the liquid to get a true reading.

The density of pure water is considered to be 1.000 at 59°F. You will probably be measuring liquids that are much warmer, in the 70°F to 90°F range, so you need to make an adjustment or correction of an additional 0.001 for every 10 degrees greater than 59°F. Thus, if your wort measures 1.035 at 90°F, then you would add 0.003 to 1.035 for an initial gravity reading of 1.038.

When you feel that fermentation is complete, take another reading. If it falls within the range given in your recipe, then you can safely bottle your beer. If not, wait a week and take another reading. If your reading falls within the given range, proceed with bottling. If it is unchanged, or remains high, then your fermentation may still be unfinished.

Assuming that your beer is finished, you can now determine how much alcohol is in it. To use your hydrometer's potential alcohol scale, simply subtract the final reading on the scale from the initial reading. You can also subtract the final gravity from the initial gravity, and multiply by 105 to get percent alcohol by weight (abw). The alcohol content of beer varies from 3 percent in low-alcohol brews to 10 or 11 percent in a serious brew. Most beers will typically be close to 5 percent alcohol.

The hydrometer that comes with the equipment kit is likely to be very delicate and requires careful handling. The first one we had broke from temperature stress while being sanitized. Some of the more expensive models are more durable. Because the hydrometer never touches the potential beer, it does not need to be sanitized, but it should be kept clean. The plastic sampling tube will need to be sanitized, unless you are using a wine thief or turkey baster to fill it (in which case, you must sanitize either of them).

NOTE: Pour the wort sample down the drain. If you return it to the fermenter, you could contaminate your beer.

SOURCES
FOR SUPPLIES AND INFORMATION

A good homebrew supply store is your most precious resource. Sure, Internet sources have exploded and yes, they may have more selection and cheaper prices. But many years of wandering in the wilderness, living off whatever we could find on the health food store back shelves, has shown us the value of local shops and expertise. The absolute best way to learn homebrewing is under the guidance of somebody who knows how, quite likely the brewguys at your local establishment. If you have access to such a place, frequent it, buy their products, and advocate it to others. We are lucky enough to have a new store, Central Street Farmhouse (207-992-4454, www. centralstreetfarmhouse.com), here in Bangor. Asa and Zeth helped us out a lot with the preparation of this edition of *Brewing Made Easy*. Thanks, guys!

Locate your nearest homebrewing supply shop by checking the local yellow pages, which should have a listing under "Brewing Supplies," "Beer — Homebrewing Supplies," or "Winemaking Supplies." Even if they do not carry what you need, they may be able to special-order it for you. Stores often host brewing classes and may offer on-premise brewing, and will often offer ready-made kits of their own tested recipes.

Another source of good information is your local homebrewing club. Most metropolitan areas now have one or more. These experienced homebrewers will be happy to share their experiences. If there is a homebrewing supply shop located near you, ask the owners if there is a club nearby. In addition, the American Homebrewers Association has a list of all the clubs in the country that are registered with it. Contact them at 888-822-6273 or on the web at www. homebrewersassociation.org.

Homebrewing magazines and their websites also have a lot to offer the new brewer. Along with lots of information, the magazines have many advertisements for dealers and manufacturers of special equipment. Start by subscribing to *Zymurgy*, the magazine of the American Homebrewers Association.

Contact them at the information given above. *Brew Your Own* magazine is another great one, published eight times a year. Contact them at 800-900-7594 or www.byo.com.

The Internet is a huge source of homebrewing info. Mailing lists, bulletin boards, and forums are free, offering lots of opportunities to ask questions and get answers. Especially for those who live in sparsely populated areas, the online services can be an excellent way to connect with other homebrewers.

Many brewers post podcasts and instructional YouTube videos on the Internet. The Brewing Network (www.thebrewingnetwork.com) has several different shows. *The Sunday Session* offers interviews with microbrewers, brewing authors, and other professionals. On *Brew Strong*, brewing authors John Palmer and Jamil Zainasheff host question-and-answer sessions with listeners and discuss the fine points of brewing technique. Jamil Zainasheff and Jon Plise create homebrewed versions of popular commercial microbrews on *The Jamil Show*.

Hosted by James Spencer and Steve Wilkes, Basic Brewing Radio (www.basicbrewing.com) presents brewing experiments, tips on brewing unusual styles of beer, road trips to places of beery interest, and stories from all levels of the hobby and industry. As its name suggests, this show is often less technical than the Brewing Network shows. Basic Brewing Video is the same show with a visual element.

Northern Brewer Homebrew Supply (800-681-2739, www.northernbrewer.com) is the largest online homebrew supplier, and offers videos and forums as well as events and classes in three Midwest brick-and-mortar locations. They also produce their own line of equipment and malt extract. Lots of other retailers (way too many to list here) have similar offerings and a simple search will turn them up.

INDEX

Page numbers in *italic* indicate illustrations: numbers in **bold** indicate charts.